Over the West Front

Over the West Front

Two Accounts of British Pilots During the
First World War in Europe

Short Flights With the Cloud Cavalry
"Spin"

Cavalry of the Clouds
"Contact"

LEONAUR

Over the West Front
Two Accounts of British Pilots During the
First World War in Europe
Short Flights With the Cloud Cavalry by "Spin"
and
Cavalry of the Clouds by "Contact"

First published under the titles
Short Flights With the Cloud Cavalry
and
Cavalry of the Clouds

Leonaur is an imprint of Oakpast Ltd

Copyright in this form © 2010 Oakpast Ltd

ISBN: 978-0-85706-047-1 (hardcover)
ISBN: 978-0-85706-048-8 (softcover)

http://www.leonaur.com

Publisher's Notes

Contents

Short Flights
With the Cloud Cavalry

"Spin"

Contents

I Dedicate
This Maiden Book
Without Permission
To Pip Beer.

Foreword

The following sketches have been written from a few odd notes made from time to time in France and other places.

Since they were written, times have changed, no longer do mist and clouds mean an indolent day spent in exploring some ancient French town; few are the hot air gaps that prevent our "intrepid aviators" (as the Press is so fond of calling them) from executing awe-inspiring stunts over the heads of our strafing enemies. Machines now fly at far lower and far higher altitudes than they did a year ago.

It is hoped that some of the sketches will awaken memories of past days in the minds of those who fly. Those who do not fly but take an interest in the art, will possibly find an insight into the lives led by those who make war at high altitudes. They may also find that pilots are in reality ordinary men, possessing the ordinary attributes of man—and a few others—and lacking in many cases—imagination.

Incidents similar to those described in the ensuing pages happen almost daily, and to those who are amused by, and who study youthful human nature, life is full of interest.

CHAPTER 1

The New World

To those endowed with an imagination, I suppose leaving the security of the warm brown earth is the most unnerving portion of the first few flights. The roar of the engine that is to bear you aloft into the new world is slightly disconcerting, and the hot smell of the castor oil which in time one gets to love is at first apt to make one feel rather sick. But these slight fancies fade away in that first rush through the morning air, when the wind stings against your face and your blood races through the veins and makes you want to laugh and sing and shout; it can only be dimly compared to the after effect of a cold bath on a healthy body. A Canadian was once asked why he took up flying. His immediate answer was, "I guess I'm a crazy mutt."

As it happened he was, but I don't think it was this that prompted him to fly. As an explorer seeks out new lands, so do many people thirst for new sensations, and in flying they find the best of all. To watch an aeroplane on a sunny day—well piloted—gracefully turning and soaring through the sunlight air, diving to the hum of the wind among the wires, slowly spiralling, answering to the slightest whim of the pilot within—it seems as if machine and man were one live thing revelling in the joy of life and being. Imagine yourself, if you can, ten thousand feet above the earth on a sunny spring morning. Imagine the even roar of the engine in front of you and the sweet fresh air stinging your face to a rosy warmth; the world stretching out like an enormous round map beneath you seems very trivial, while you, the master of the air, swoop and dive so far above it. The sun is all around you; it glints and shines on the whirling propeller in front and lights the world with loveliness beneath you.

Green pastures cut by silver streams and tiny woods are stretching far away to the misty blur of the twinkling sea. On and on you rush, while the world beneath seems to slide slowly away. It is hard to realise that you are travelling about ninety miles an hour. Tiny towns and villages come and pass behind you, and all the world is intersected by narrow yellow lanes turning and twisting from the long straight roads on which the antlike vehicles seem stationary. A ghostly cloud, like a puff of smoke, glides by; another and larger one appears, in front a twist—a sudden bank, and you leave it far behind.

Away to the left great rolls of thunder clouds mass heavy and solid—the sunshine falls athwart them in golden pencils, lighting the shadowed ground beneath in uneven circles. It's time to roost. The sun starts tinting the fleecy clouds with rosy smudges and the world beneath grows dim and shadowy. The streams appear like rivers of running blood. Slowly the great red sun sinks in a blaze behind the violet hills. A sudden hush as the pilot "switches off" gives way to the rushing hum of the wires and the whistle of the propeller. Down goes the nose of the machine and the world grows rapidly larger and more stable in the quick descent; the wires hum louder and louder as the speed increases, until the machine seems to shriek with a protest of being forced from its high command.

Then from a gentle spiral you come out above the aerodrome, glide down and bump to a gentle standstill. Back again in the old world life seems very slow, and one vaguely gets that sensation of solidity and reality that meets one coming out of a theatre into the cold and rainy streets.

The Day

There was so much to do and so much to be thought of that it was not until one got into bed the night before the first day that one wondered what it was going to be like.

"I wonder what Archie feels like," said James, my pilot, from a pile of blankets the other side of the hut.

I put the light out and curling up in my bed beneath a mass of coats and rugs, thought of the day that was almost gone. Looking back, it seemed to be weeks ago that my servant had knocked on my door and reminded me that in half an hour I was to fly over to France. Then came the packing, the unpacking to find one's flying cap, the last look at the hut, the last breakfast eaten off packing crates, and then the start.

It had been a perfect day, and one had looked down rather wistfully at the sunlit English fields and villages speeding away far below and the faint line of sparkling blue away to the south—that narrow strip of water that divides so much—and then came the landing at Dymstone, the donning of enormous and exceedingly uncomfortable lifebelts, the shrieks of mirth at little fat McJim, our youngest pilot, because he looked so much wider than he was tall, and the hurried lunch of chocolate and biscuits.

The major "took off" and one by one we followed him, climbing and turning until we all had got our height and had fallen into place in the formation. Reluctantly we turned our eyes from the white cliffs and the red roofs of Dymstone, and faced the misty line of the unknown land across the stretch of blue sea. Here and there a tiny black destroyer raced through the water, leaving two great lines of white surf behind, but beyond these there was very little to break the sheet of blue. For a quarter of an hour we had droned our way along towards the unknown, watching the misty line become more real, until it slowly revealed a land of long straight roads and green undulating fields. We crossed a town and a mass of canals stretching their long arms to the south, east and west. A little later came the landing at the depot, stamping and waving our arms we drove out the cold waiting for the others and sniffing the strange, unfamiliar air of France. A machine appeared a black speck far away. "I bet that's Billy," said McJim, and critically we watched the landing. "It can't be Billy," said someone, "it's far too good," and when the machine "taxied" up, Billy's rosy face beamed out at us with a satisfied grin.

Only two machines had failed to arrive on account of engine trouble in England, and in two tenders we drove down to O——.

After an amazingly good lunch at the Vin d'Or we again set out, and as the daylight began to fade we arrived at our final destination.

Then came the scramble for huts and the looting of past owners' property.

At half-past six the major summoned us to the office and detailed four machines for patrol the following morning. We were not to make ourselves offensive, but just to spy out the land.

As the transport hadn't yet arrived we dined off boxes, listening to the unfamiliar rumble of guns and feeling that the war was very near. Eight of us thought a good deal of the morning.

I think we were all fairly tired, and after a few reminiscences purposely made kind from the pilots who had been out before, we wandered off to unpack and smoke a last cigarette before getting into bed.

The last inmate had left the hut, I was sharing with Jimmy, in fairly good order. We surmised that he had left in a hurry, as the windows possessed curtains, and most of the floor was covered with mats. There was also a chair and a table, and the inevitable "Kitchener" faces simpered down at us in large quantities from the walls.

"I wonder what Archie feels like?" said Jimmy sleepily. I wondered too, and fell asleep thinking of a house in a little English village and a white-haired lady.

CHAPTER 3

Archie

After breakfast on the aerodrome next morning we had our first sight of aerial hate. A dull sound of crumping made us look to the east—the sky was covered in one part with a cloud of soft, black woolly balls which gradually expanded and faded away. A machine seemed to be almost in the middle of it, and we momentarily expected to see it burst into flames and fall in pieces—but nothing happened and Archie soon stopped.

"Ten o'clock, Walter!" said Jimmy in a decided voice. We got into the machine and settled down.

At seven thousand feet we gazed with extraordinary interest at the trenches and hole-marked swamp around them, little bursts of white smoke appeared here and there and slowly drifted away in the breeze. There was no sign of life anywhere.

An appalling explosion behind me made me turn like lightning. Two large clouds of smoke about fifty feet away, and another nearer and on the right, for a moment staggered me—and then—"Archie!" I yelled to Jimmy. Jimmy turned and beamed at me and side slipped vigorously. The next Archie was far above us and in front, Jimmy again turned and beamed, and I nodded and felt that Archie was nothing to be alarmed at at all.

A few minutes later, as I was watching a machine some distance over the lines being pursued by the black explosions, one suddenly burst right underneath it, the machine faltered for a moment, side slipped, and spun down with a long riband of flame streaking out behind it. My confidence seemed to subside, and again I felt that Archie was a thing to take quite seriously.

Every machine that came near us made me feel uneasy until I spotted the red, white and blue circles, and then they comforted me as nothing else in the air can.

Two of the other three machines had met Huns; they were very full of their brief scraps, and the ante-room was a babel of voices as we entered. The fourth machine had got two small shrapnel holes in their planes, and its occupants were making as much noise as if they had been shot down in flames and come out of it unscathed.

Jimmy and I were the only ones who had nothing to talk about, so we drowned the rest with vivid stories from our imaginations, and I can still see our elderly and innocent Australian pilot of "30," wide-eyed and staring, ejaculating breathlessly, "*Nooooo, reely??*" as we told him how the shells had passed in pairs between our struts.

The "first crump" is always the worst, and as time goes on familiarity breeds very nearly contempt, and one learns to avoid the whining buzz of broken shrapnel which, to the pilot fresh from home, is distinctly embarrassing.

CHAPTER 4

Those Indispensable People

There are few squadrons that do not possess a mechanical maniac—a familiar figure and a general nuisance in the workshop lorries—a figure whose hair is never brushed, whose clothes are in the last state of decay and whose hands are only clean at meal times, and not always then. Enter his hut and you will find it a mass of gadgets, wireless parts, wheels, old aerials and a thousand devices which never function. His conversation is incoherent with long technical words, and he'll explain how anything works from a magneto to a tramway car without the slightest provocation. His family must have a rotten time when he's at home, but he's usually, a very good fellow at heart.

Another type is the squadron lunatic, an invaluable being, his face is very often sufficient to drive away that trying attack of dyspepsia. His imitations, his irresponsible actions, his love of laughter and practical joking, his apparent childishness—all make one rather fearful of endangering one's life in a frail construction of wood and fabric 10,000 feet above the earth with him as pilot—but he's as steady and as capable as any man when there's a man's job to be done. And, then, we have the War Baby. These strange creatures are beginning to abound in most Squadrons. The big blue eyes, the red baby mouth, the smooth cheek innocent of razors nearly always give the impression of great innocence, but in reality beneath these attractions lies the most diabolical cunning, and they can very often lead the old hand through the many and delicate hot air paths which abound in the life of an aviator. They make admirable girls for the local *pierrot troupes*, and sometimes create the most amusing *contre-temps*.

The "*affaire*" of the dashing officer who fell violently in love with the leading "lady" of an amateur *troupe* is still warm in the hearts of the many who were present when this particular War Baby pulled off his wig and discomfited the admirer. The unfortunate fellow is still wondering whether he carried it off all right. Another indispensable is the cock-tail manufacturer. His sacred hour is the hour before mess. From many bottles of all sizes and shapes he produces liquids of the most violent colours and mysterious tastes, which he solemnly avers are at that moment creating "furores" in town or New York, or wherever is the natural home of the cocktail.

His interest in his work never flags, and one is invariably greeted on entering the ante-room by cries of "Come and try the 'Health-and-Strength'; What! you've never heard of it—Good Lord, where were you dragged up?" Of course one has never heard of it, because he's only just created it by upsetting something on the floor and sweeping it up into a glass. Then there's the piano player—not the instrument you play hurriedly upon with your feet, but the fellow who can sit down at the piano and play anything from a classic opera to a very much syncopated fox-trot or an unconventional song of doubtful origin, or accompany an artiste on a squadron-made violin.

He is the most indispensable of the lot, and many a French peasant has listened from his cottage door to the volume of sound—the roar of many voices emitted from a Flying Mess—Somewhere in France in celebration of some great event—such as the full moon or another Hun brought down. Can it still be said the English take their pleasures sadly? I wonder.

CHAPTER 5

The Fear of Fear

"Nerves! Ransom hasn't any nerves. He's the stoutest fellow in my flight." The three flight commanders were sitting in a hut one summer night discussing their individual flights. Rivalry was always apt to be a little rampant when the three got on to the subject of their individual pilots. "I tell you Ransom hasn't got a nerve in his body," continued the tallest of the three emphatically. "If I had the slightest doubt I'd get him back to Blighty at once—his time's up tomorrow anyway, but we can't spare him you know just yet." The subject of their conversation was sitting alone in his hut, his head resting miserably on his hands, and in his mind was an awful fear—the fear of himself, the fear that he might show it. He got up and paced slowly up and down, and taking a cigarette lit it with a trembling hand. Suddenly he stopped, and opening the door looked up at the clear and starlit sky.

A fleecy cloud or two sped across the face of the round white moon, and away in the East the dull roar of guns and the tiny points of red light in the sky hastened some bomb-dropping flight on its way into Hunland. With a slight shiver he turned and closed the door. Someone suddenly knocked. Ransom started. "Come in."

An orderly entered. "Captain Brewster wants you. Sir, for a moment in his hut."

Ransom nodded casually. "All right, Jones." The orderly saluted and closed the door. Ransom's breath came in quick, short jerks. Lighting another cigarette he opened the door and strolled out into the night.

Brewster was alone, and smiled when Ransom entered. "I say, old thing, I'm awfully sorry, but I've got to go to O—— tomorrow, and I want you to lead that photographic stunt for me."

Ransom blew out a cloud of smoke and nodded, "Right, Brewster, what time?"

The flight commander plunged into details and explanations. "You feel all right. Old Bean, don't you?" he said as Ransom was leaving.

Ransom laughed. "Rather—fit as Hell." . . .

"Six o'clock, sir, and a fine morning." The orderly drew aside the blind and let in a stream of sunshine. Ransom opened tired eyes with a feeling of stifling oppression and got slowly out of bed. He dressed and looked out of the window. The sky was clear but over the salient a thick black pall seemed to hang like a curtain shutting out the hideous drama of a ceaseless war.

He drank the cup of steaming tea that his servant had brought, and taking his flying cap and goggles walked slowly across the aerodrome. Four machines were drawn out in front of the sheds, while mechanics busied themselves with finishing taps and adjustments.

One by one the seven other aviators came across and gathered round Ransom. "It's still pretty dud over the salient." Ransom nodded.

"Well, wait a bit." Eight o'clock came and the curtain began to lift as the sun got higher. Ransom was walking up and down the tarmac, kicking stones in front of him. Archie began to get busy, and balloons slowly rose till their heads nodded against the low-drifting clouds.

Ransom's heart was beating fast. It was now or never. With a jerk he dropped his cigarette and climbed into his machine.

In the office the major, pencil in hand, was listening to the wing adjutant attempting to say something through the deafening rattles, buzzes, sighs and moans that accompany one's voice through the telephone. "Hullo, yes, Dickson, Nottingham, and Ransom to be transferred to Home Establishment on the 22nd. Right. . . ."

Four machines in perfect formation cautiously crossed the trenches. A strong west wind was blowing and, although Archie saw them well—he observed the direction of the wind and maintained a discreet silence, waiting for the return journey, when they would come struggling against the wind to form a perfect target. Such is Archie's little subterfuge.

He pretends when he sees you coming that many failures have made him sulky and that he's not even going to try for you, and thus he fancies the innocent young aviator is lured far over the line, but when the machine turns to go home against an adverse wind, Archie springs to life with many a "crump" and snarl. The four machines quickly found their objective and took their souvenirs. Perfectly they turned together and crump, crump, crump banged the Archie amongst them. Four observers, their guns ready, scanned the blue for cross-marked enemies. Four pilots, their faith in their engines, divided their time between hasty looks at their instruments and rapid glances around the sky. Ransom crouching in his machine, started hopelessly at every "crump"; his eyes were on the distant trenches, and he cursed the strong west wind. His observer, Robin, glanced calmly round the sky with the air of one who commands the situation and is satisfied with the world in general.

Part of the time he spent in jocular messages to which Ransom nodded, but paid no attention. "Crump-clang," the machine reeled from the shock, hesitated and plunged forward again. Ransom crouched lower and peered round for the three other machines. Two were following close behind. One rather lagged. Suddenly Archie stopped and Robin looking up, saw away above them an enormous number of machines, glittering white in the sun. He caught his breath. "Gawd, the circus!" he whispered and steadied his gun.

Ransom with a rapid glance over his shoulder saw them too. Quickly raising the Very pistol, he fired a light.

The whole formation turned and as they turned, nine of the enemy machines dived. *Staccato* cracks tore splinters round them and ripped jagged holes along their fabric. The formation soon broke up and individual fighting started. Ransom fired his forward gun straight into the gleaming belly of a black-crossed machine banking before him.

The bullets were flashing straight into it, and emotionless he saw it side-slip and spin quickly down. Crack, crack, crack. The bullets tore and whipped about him, splashing the wood around his eyes.

Robin behind was firing in rapid bursts, cool-handed and steady. From the corner of his eye Ransom saw two machines flashing down in flames and smoke. Pulling the machine round he side-slipped, spun her down 1,000 feet, pulled her out again and quickly looked around.

Far away he saw a group of machines hastening back to Hunland, but of the other three of his formation he saw nothing. He looked behind. Robin was quietly tying bandages round his wrist, his face beneath his goggles rather white.

Half an hour later—they were on the aerodrome. Two of the other three machines were there and one of the observers lay dying in the medical hut. Ransom hastened to the office to make his report.

The major looked up with a relieved expression when he entered.

"I heard about your scrap, Ransom, from an R.E. 8. Did you see poor old Dickson shot down?"

Ransom, his face white and his hand tightening and untightening convulsively, spoke slowly. "I think I must have seen him spinning down on the top of a Hun, but I couldn't be sure, sir. I think we got two altogether. Yes, sir, it was the circus."

The major suddenly looked up. "By the way. Ransom, you've to go home tomorrow."

Ransom swayed slightly, saluted, and walked out unsteadily from the office.

CHAPTER 6

A Daily Round

"Nice bright flying day, sir." Jimmy rolled over, opened his eyes and looked with much venom at his servant. It was just seven, and, as Jimmy's servant had remarked, it was a perfect Spring morning, clear and frosty and the sky a stretch of unbroken blue. Jimmy got out of bed yawning, and put his two shivering legs into a large pair of comforting fleece-lined thigh boots, and started the difficult process of shaving on a cold day with a tender skin and lukewarm water. "Wish I was in the Navy," he sighed, as a small red streak by his chin denoted that the daily loss of blood had started—and he looked with envy at the photograph of his naval brother who was adorned with a young and promising beard. Presently the door opened and Nichol, his observer, entered whistling. "By Jove, what a ghastly fug in here!" Jimmy murmured a protest.

Nichol advanced, and taking a cigarette from Jimmy's box sat down heavily on the bed. "Are you aware, my lad, that we are indulging in the so-called pastime of air-fighting at 8.30 ack-emma, and it's now 7.45." Jimmy *was* aware, and said so forcibly. At 8.15 they were both on the Aerodrome. All the machines were out before the Sheds, and one with a loud increasing roar was just skimming along the grass "taking off." Far away to the East half-a-dozen Observation balloons hung motionless, and still further a small machine hurried along, pursued by the inevitable little black bursts of Archie apparently absorbed in a "shoot." On the way to their shed Jimmy and Nichol met two others laden with maps, and arguing violently as to the individual merits of high-explosive Archie over shrapnel. Jimmy frowned at them.

"For Gawd's sake stop talking hot air, my lads, and don't foul the beautiful morning." The two laughed, and retorted with an expressive but impolite *repartee*. At one o'clock the mess was full of people discussing the morning's work, and the continuation of it in the afternoon.

Jimmy and Nichol had succeeded beyond their wildest hopes, and had removed two Hun batteries. There were very few Huns about, and only lack of petrol and hunger had stayed them from demolishing a third. At two o'clock the frequent roar of engines, gradually fading away in the distance, again left the Aerodrome nearly empty.

One machine was left. In it Jimmy was moaning "Contact" for the umpteenth time, and Nichol in the back seat was languidly watching a succession of perspiring mechanics vainly endeavouring to start the engine.

The major suddenly appeared. "Hullo, not off yet?" Jimmy shouted dismally, " No, sir, the engine's dud—she was missing a bit this morning." The major took hold of the propeller and shouted "Contact!"

"Contact!" echoed Jimmy. A spluttering roar, which gradually settled to a steady drone, and they were away bounding over the grass towards the East. The major often managed to succeed when others failed. At half-past five the light started to fade, and away in the West great banks of rain clouds were gathering. Most of the machines were back, and were being pushed into their sheds by attendant mechanics hot of face and language. Only two were still "up." At six-fifteen the light was getting dim, and far away a distant drone brought the mechanics out to gaze up into the violet sky. "That's Captain Renfel," said one mechanic. "Aye, it's time that Mester James was doon," said Jimmy's rigger.

In the office the major was listening to a multitude of ghostly voices, cracks and buzzes jambing the telephone. "Hullo, hullo, is that the Wireless? Has Mr. James finished his shoot?"

A pause. "Yes, sir, he gave the signal at 5.30."

The major wrinkled his forehead. "Thank you." Picking up a Very pistol he went out on to the aerodrome, fired a light up into the falling night, and looked away towards the East. Again he fired and listened. Far away a little light high up in the sky burst and fell in a shower of stars. Ten minutes later Jimmy and Nichol were explaining exactly how they had taken the wrong turning and lost their way, and how they had succeeded once again in "putting the wind up" a Hun battery and had spoilt three of their guns. Away in the distance the guns flashed and rumbled, and from the mess came the sound of many people all talking at once. "Come on old Bean and change," said Jimmy, taking his observer's arm. The daily round was done.

CHAPTER 7

"365"

"It's becoming positively childish," said the major, as a small aviator passed the window with a large silver mascot dangling from his identity bracelet, and turning with a frown to an orderly told him that he wanted to see Mr. McGuy, then he sat down at his table and prepared for an offensive. Ten minutes later McGuy came out of the office looking worried, and the bracelet on his wrist was conspicuous by the absence of ornament. McGuy looked unhappy for the greater part of the evening, and before going to bed unburdened his sorrowful soul to Jimmy. "It's too childish for words," he said, unconsciously reiterating the major's words. "She only sent it to me two days ago—anyway, I'm going to carry it with me tomorrow." Words failed him, and Jimmy looked appropriately sympathetic. McGuy, with an angry glance at the sky, retired to his hut to brood in solitude over the foibles of superior officers.

Before getting into bed he placed with tender care two small objects on the table by his bed. One was a silver bulldog with enormous bulging eyes and a large smile; the other was a locket. Before turning out the light he opened the latter and looked for a few moments at the photograph within, and turning over on his side nestled his head in the pillow and was soon asleep. McGuy was just eighteen and very young for his age—or was he old? One never quite knew.

The following morning a breathless flight commander shattered an extraordinarily satisfactory dream of a very long leave, in which a wealthy and altruistic uncle, a pretty girl, and himself were the principal characters. "I say, McGuy, the flight sergeant tells me your engine must come out, they tried to patch it up, but I'm afraid it's had its day—you'd better take 365."

McGuy awoke and opened his mouth wide. "Oh I say, Brewster,

29

isn't there another machine? You know 365 is the unluckiest in the squadron."

The flight commander laughed. "365 is all right, it's only the people who can't fly that give it its bad reputation."

McGuy sighed. "Right—Brewster."

At ten o'clock that morning McGuy and his observer sat in No. 365—the last machine on the aerodrome. The observer felt uncomfortable, and missed the "gadgets" which he had fixed all round him in his own machine. McGuy, with a resigned expression, was shouting "Contact!" for the eighth time. Eventually the engine started, and McGuy watched the rev-counter with an unexpectant eye; however, when he opened out the engine he seemed surprised, and after a moment or two waved his right hand. "The chocs" were pulled away from the wheels, and two mechanics, their hair waving in the draught from the propeller, lifted the tail and turned the machine. Over the lines—the engine was going well, and McGuy became interested in the shoot. He watched the little white bursts creeping round and nearer the target, while the observer, his right hand on the wireless key and a pencil in the left, fixed his eyes on the wood and guided the bursting shells. Nearer and nearer the shells crept, until they were bursting on the target. It was just at this point that the engine, without the faintest splutter, stopped.

The observer signalled down to the battery to continue to fire in their own time, and sat back patiently in his seat. McGuy turned the nose of the machine towards home and glided softly along—trying everything he knew to coax the engine back to life again. They were dropping rapidly, and the observer began to wind up the aerial. McGuy swore. They were well over the line, but only 500 feet up, and had eight miles to go to get to the nearest aerodrome. He rapidly unbuckled his belt; then remembering that he had heard someone say it was wiser to crash with one's belt buckled, he quickly did it up again. His observer was sitting back in his seat quietly watching the ground beneath growing rapidly nearer. McGuy, with a quick look, spotted a fairly large field which seemed clear of the inevitable hop-poles, and S—— turned steeply down. His observer took off his goggles, thrust them in his pocket, and cautiously held on to the sides of the machine.

With a long-drawn swish and a whistle they glided over the head of an astonished peasant—a slight bump—another—and McGuy suddenly saw a small deep ditch in front.

He pulled the joy stick feverishly in an attempt to "Jump it." There was a sudden jolt, and the universe seemed to meet and mingle in a dizzy crash!

The next moment McGuy found himself crouching in an uncomfortable attitude upside down in a very confined space—a smell of hot oil around him, and a bruise growing painfully and rapidly into an enormous bump.

He crawled out—simultaneously with the dejected figure of his Observer. They met on all fours, and looked pathetically at each other. "Damn and blast," said McGuy, and he glanced down at his bracelet bereft of ornament. "Confound it," he said, adding other expressive and comforting words—"I knew I'd forget the blasted thing!"

CHAPTER 8

"Hot Air Gaps"

Two o'clock in the afternoon, and the sky still covered by low heavy clouds. In the mess hut everything was peaceful; in ten large armchairs ten youthful-looking aviators were sleeping off an after-lunch coma. Every face suggested satisfaction, every attitude repose—not a sound broke the stillness of a perfectly dud day. The door opened and an orderly entered, hesitated and coughed noisily.

"Mr. Morelux, sir." Ten youthful pilots stirred uneasily in their sleep. One yawned and opened his eyes. The orderly saluted. "Mr. Morelux, you're wanted at once at the office." Morelux, a fair-haired youth with a shamefully young face, leaped to his feet, strode anxiously to the window and inspected the sky. The result appeared to make him anxious.

"Lord, it's getting fine," he murmured in a sepulchral tone. These few words, which under ordinary circumstances would have gladdened the hearts of most people, produced the most extraordinary commotion in this particular mess room. The nine aviators instantly woke up, sprang to their feet, hurling remarks which were not endearing at the pilot who had broken their slumber so unfeelingly. "Rot, liar. Good God, it's true," burst in an unanimous howl from nine throats.

"There are some more clouds coming up over there," remarked an optimist at another window. Instantly the crowd surged to the optimist's window and peered up anxiously.

"Well, our tea at H—— is washed out anyhow," wailed three pilots, whose combined ages couldn't have amounted to more than 57.

As Morelux seized his hat and strode to the door an orderly entered. "All officers wanted at once at the office, sir." Archant, the squadron lunatic, started to give an imitation of a dog objecting to a piano solo, but was submerged by the combined rush for the door.

In the office the major stood by his table, a telephone glued to his ear, a pencil in one hand, a list of targets in the other and a large map before him on the table. His face always wore an anxious look.

The three flight commanders with their flying coats on were bending over the map on the table muttering incoherently.

As Morelux entered the major was talking mysteriously down the telephone, "Pip one ack two and Don four. Yes, it's rather far over, but we'll do it if we can."

Morelux experienced that quaint sinking sensation and crept behind a large map box. "Don four," he murmured to himself. "Lord, why not do a shoot on Berlin while we're about it?" The next moment the remainder of the squadron, roused from their couches by breathless orderlies, dashed in, and the office at once became a seething mass of people in flying coats, maps and photographs. All spoke quickly of strange things. "We'll go up to Pip, then follow down to ack five, you start taking them there. Yes, get four o.k.s., then we'll wait about half an hour after 6.0, and if they're firing all right we'll push off."

"Where's Slow?" wailed a dark curly-headed lad. "Where's my perfectly well-formed observer, Slow? Slow?" The door opened and Slow entered laden with a young clothes' shop and five maps, which he proceeded to scatter in different parts of the office, much to the Adjutant's disgust. Morelux and his observer, a remarkably tall, thin fellow with perfectly brushed hair, whose *sobriquet* was a "Stream-line," was bending over a map, giving each other last injunctions, "And don't forget," Morelux was saying, "if you see a Hun, don't go on with your shoot as you did last time; give me two hits on the head, and we'll give him Hades."

Outside the sky was fairly clear, and the sun was shining in an anaemic fashion through a faint mist on the machines drawn out in front of the sheds. Mechanics were hurriedly looking over the cameras and aerials, and giving last taps and twists to engines. In ten minutes all the aviators were in their machines. Morelux, whose flying coat, sweater, and various other protections against the cold made him look like an elderly gentleman in the last stage of dropsy, climbed into the machine.

"Petrol on, switch off, suck in!" "The mechanic turned the propeller round, and the engine sighed like some huge animal waking up.

"Contact!" shouted the ack-emma. Morelux looked back over his shoulder. "All right, Jimmy."

"All right," echoed his observer. The pilot pulled down his goggles.

"Contact!" The mechanic gave the propeller a lusty heave, and with a roar the engine started. Morelux looked at his rev-counter all serene, and throttling down the machine was about to "taxi" out, when an orderly ran out.

"Wash out, sir," he screamed.

Morelux throttled down until the propeller was just ticking over. "What's that?"

"Wash out, sir," repeated the orderly; shouting, "The major says it's not good enough." Jimmy looked up at the sky. The gap had gone, and again the sky was covered with low, heavy, fast flying clouds. He switched off, and made a curious signal to his observer.

He turned both his thumbs up. "Come on, Jimmy." And the mechanic pushed the machine back into the shed, and on their faces they wore large smiles.

CHAPTER 9

An Orderly-Dog's Day

Jimmy, having successfully turned out the guard, was sitting in a pair of pink pyjamas on his bed warming his feet by the stove, when someone knocked loudly at the door. "Come in," shouted Jimmy, stifling a yawn.

A corporal entered and saluted. "There's a machine, sir, been firing lights over the aerodrome. It went away, and now it's coming back, sir. Had we better fire some lights?"

Jimmy jumped off the bed and started to pull on a pair of thigh boots over his pyjamas, muttering imprecations against over-zealous and tactless bomb-droppers. "Poop off some lights, corporal, and light the flares."

The corporal saluted, "Very good, sir," and ran off. Jimmy, yawning loudly, slipped on a heavy flying coat and opened the door. A frosty wind met him, and made him look reluctantly back at the warm little stove in the hut.

"Curse these night-flying idiots," he said unfeelingly, and seizing an electric torch ran along the road towards the aerodrome. Except for the occasional pop of the Very pistol, the night was very still. A few stars twinkled dimly through the cold mist which hung in heavy shrouds around the trees and ditches. The corporal and two other men were standing by the guard hut staring up into the night, and several dim figures in the middle of the aerodrome were arranging the flickering flares.

Jimmy ran up to the corporal, "Seen any more lights. corporal?"

The corporal pointed away to the East—a tiny ball appeared high up in the gloom, fell in a little red streak, and faded in a burst of stars. "There she is, sir."

Jimmy took the pistol from the corporal and pulled the trigger. A light shot up, burst, and fell in a shower of stars. They could hear the machine now, the regular tick-a- tack, tick-a-tack, accompanied by a low drone was getting louder and louder—the little group on the aerodrome stared up, trying to pierce the deep black gloom.

Suddenly the drone ceased and gave place to the musical whine of the wind through wires. "She's coming down all right," said Jimmy, "it's a Fe I think," and ran out on to the aerodrome. The whining note got softer and nearer as the machine "S"— turned and gradually slowed preparatory to landing. All of a sudden, like a grey ghost, it shot out of the darkness with a whistle and bumped softly to a standstill. Jimmy ran up to it, and as he got near the pilot shouted to him, "*Wo bin Ich?*"

"I beg your pardon," said Jimmy politely. A stream of German oaths polluted the night, and Jimmy's heart for a moment ceased to function. He was up against the machine, and quickly recognised one of Germany's latest scouts. The pilot fumbled in his pocket for something, but Jimmy was quicker. "Put your damned hands up," he yelled excitedly, pointing the pistol a foot away from the pilot's nose. "Leave your pocket alone, and get out."

The pilot looked for a moment down at the boyish determined face, and at the pistol, and with a slight shrug of his shoulders climbed out and removed his flying cap. The guard were by this time standing round the two—fingering their rifles dangerously. Jimmy waved them aside, and advancing towards the Hun, who as far as he could see in the gloom was a tall, rather heavy sort of individual, grasped and shook his astonished hand. Jimmy never quite understood what prompted him to do this—probably because he was so relieved to find that the Hun "came quietly," so to speak. Half an hour later Jimmy was lying on his bed, while eighteen pilots in various stages of *négligé* were trying to get into the hut, which measured six feet by ten. Everyone was talking at once, except Jimmy, who sipped a large whisky and soda slowly and very self-consciously.

CHAPTER 10

Ack-Emma

(A.M., *I.E.* AIR MECHANIC)

Thomson was very Scotch. His accent was Scotch, his conscience was Scotch, his hair was red, and his simplicity childlike. This is all that anyone could discover about Thomson; he kept very much to himself. His duty was to keep Morelux's engine in form, and his sole ambition seemed to be to prevent the engine from letting Morelux down, from which it may be seen that Thomson was considerably devoted to Morelux, besides having a strong sense of duty.

Thomson looked upon the engine as a live thing, and sometimes on a cold morning when it sighed and coughed but refused to start, Thomson would frown at it with a worried look, and dope it with petrol as if he were dosing a sick child with medicine.

Morelux hardly needed to test the revolutions before starting off on a job. He would climb in, Stilter would nonchalantly take his place in the back seat. "Contact, sir?" Thomson would say, patting the prop.

"Contact!" echoed Morelux; then with a roar they'd be off. Thomson would stand like a statue, his hand shading his eyes, watching the machine grow smaller and smaller until it disappeared into the morning mist, and then when it could be seen no more he would turn towards the shed with a worried look, and busy himself savagely until the faint drone high overhead brought him running out again. With the instinct bred of long practise, he could recognise his own machine when other ack-emmas could barely tell the species.

And then when Morelux returned again to the aerodrome, Thomson, his worried look gone, would run out swiftly and steady the machine back to the sheds. When Morelux climbed out of the machine, Thomson would be waiting for him. "Weel, surr," Thomson would query, well knowing what the answer would be. Morelux would smile, "Oh, she went fine, Thomson."

Then one day something happened; Morelux had been up three and a-half hours, and still there was no sign of him. Thomson stood outside the shed, alternately biting his nails and glancing back towards the office.

The flight commander appeared, "Mr. Morelux not back yet, Thomson?"

Thomson shook his head slowly. "No, surr," and continued to scan the sky, which was slowly turning violet in the twilight. Seven o'clock, it was almost dark. Very lights would suddenly pop, race up in long yellow lines, and burst into a shower of light. At half-past seven Thomson had no nails left on his right hand, and his eyes were misty. "I'm thinking they'll be doon," he said, turning with a look of despair to the Flight Sergeant as if the thought had only just struck him.

"Is Flight Sergeant Jones there?" A breathless orderly dashed up and thrust a piece of yellow paper into the flight's hand. Jones looked at it, and, passing it on to Thomson, ran off to the transport shed. On the paper was written, "No. 635 forced landing half mile N. of ——. Pilot and observer unhurt; undercarriage and prop. broken; take engineman and rigger and get there as soon as possible. Tell Mr. Morelux he is not to fly back tonight. O.C, *Umpteen* Squadron."

Thomson's breath whistled out in a long pent-up sigh of relief. "Ha'e got a gasper, laddie!" he said, turning to the rigger.

CHAPTER 11

Bumps

"Malbrouck s'en va" en air.
"Ne sait quand il revient."

"Are you ready, Parker?" said the general with a faint note of regret, as he surveyed the debris of an immodest repast.

The A.D.C. at once busied himself with cap, wraps and stick. "Is the car ready, Parker?"

"Yes, sir."

"You know, Parker," continued the general facetiously, "it may be the last time we'll have the opportunity of using it."

Parker gave a harsh duty laugh and shuddered involuntarily. The general, temporarily rejuvenated by the Spring air, had decided to experience his first flight. A few minutes later the heavy car glided softly to a throbbing standstill on the edge of a large aerodrome. "Good morning, Major," said the general, stepping heavily out of the car on to the toe of the A.D.C., who winced but maintained a tactful silence.

The squadron commander raised his hand to his flying cap, and conducted the general slowly and reverently round the sheds. Presently they came to a machine which was swaying slightly to the breeze —mechanics busy round the engine. "Would you care to go up now, sir, or will you wait a bit?"

"Yes, yes, quite ready."

"Right, sir," said the major, handing him a flying cap and a pair of goggles.

"Thank ye—thank ye," said the general, attempting to put the cap on upside down. "Yes, yes, of course. Let's see now, how do we get in? Eh?"

Two mechanics gently raised him into the seat. "Dear me," said the general, "what a very confined space!"

"Contact!" shouted the major. The engine spluttered and roared, and a farewell epigram, which the general had been thinking out for the last twelve hours, was torn from his breathless lips and hurled away by the whistling draught. "Flick!"—away went the general's goggles.

"Here, stop—Hi!" The general thumped the major's broad back, the engine was throttled down to a murmur, and a panting orderly ran up with the goggles. "Should I not—" started the general, but again the engine roared out, and the screaming wind killed the epigram before it was born. Fifteen minutes later the machine landed, and the general—a clutching figure in the back seat—was assisted out.

"Very nice—very nice indeed—most enjoyable. Thanks very much, Major —— Yes—afraid I must be going. Goodbye." The door of the car slammed, and the major raised his hand to the salute. For several minutes the general was very quiet, and the A.D.C. glanced at him out the corner of a watery eye.

"Stop the car," said the general suddenly. The A.D.C. with a fluttering heart tapped the window. The general climbed unsteadily out and walked slowly down the road, his head bowed on the rows of coloured ribbons across his breast.

"Damn!" said the general, stopping. "Damn!" he said, as he was sick again.

Crashes and Landings

They may be amusing, they may be serious, or they may merely be annoying. For instance, a pilot enters the ante-room on some wet and windy day and remarks casually as he picks up the morning paper, "Archant's just run into the bomb store again." Few people raise their heads from their papers—it's probably such a common occurrence that it's ceased to be amusing, but to Archant's rigger and fitter it's more than annoying—they lead a dog's life.

Then again, owing to the fact that a couple of mechanics are being re-rigged, a new pilot borrows your machine and looks for worms by flying straight into the ground! It's very trying.

There are few things so interesting as watching a machine land. The worse the day the more interesting it becomes.

I have seen a machine make as many as seven attempts to land on a windy day, only to turn "ack. tock." (absolutely turtle) on the eighth. Sometimes one sits quietly in the ante-room—as quietly as one can sit with a gramophone asking in loud and raucous tones "*if you've seen the ducks go by,*" with two couples dancing a frenzied fox-trot, and a third couple emulating Hackenschmidt and Madrali in a corner—with four or five other people behaving like a football scrum in another corner. I say one is sitting quietly in the ante-room when the door bursts open and a dishevelled officer dashes in with, "I say, there's an S—— coming down," and disappears as violently as he appeared.

Instantly the ante-room becomes a scene of indescribable confusion, and in thirty seconds only about two very languid and blase aviators remain. The crowd surges out on to the aerodrome, and in almost breathless silence watch the landing.

If it's a good one the air is filled with long-drawn ohs and ahs—if it's a bad one, and he crashes or carries away the office, the abuse is

41

quite horrible to listen to (especially from those who happen to be in the office at the time), and the crowd advances either to inspect the new machine or the remains of it as the case may be—— or disperse to the ante-room to criticize the landing or continue the fox trot. A new pilot always affords a lot of interest, and more often than not a good deal of amusement, on his first flight in a strange squadron. Naturally he is intent on making a favourable impression on the other pilots; who very often make him slightly nervous—the results sometimes being rather unsatisfactory so far as the new pilot is concerned.

There is something very attractive about a perfect landing—to see the machine humming far above the aerodrome, the roar suddenly ceasing as it glides almost silently down in a slow steady spiral to the soft music of the wind through the wires, and in one long swoop glides down and skims along the ground until the wheels gently touch the grass, and with a few tiny bumps slows down and stops. A bad landing is not so attractive. The machine spirals down, and skims along about ten feet above the ground until it gradually slows down, and After a series of gigantic bumps and crashes—resembling a giant grasshopper—it comes to rest in a maimed condition, unable very often to pursue the uneven tenor of its way to the sheds, where it has to be ignominiously assisted back by many frowning and cursing mechanics. Sometimes it is merely picked up in pieces. The story of the great aviator who was expected at a certain aerodrome at a certain time is an old one. At two o'clock a hum was heard high above the clouds. The contents of the ante-room emptied itself upon the aerodrome to watch the arrival.

Slowly and well he spiralled down, executing a few awe-inspiring stunts on the way, and until he was about a hundred feet up the spectators stood quietly in silent admiration, and then it suddenly became obvious the great man was intent on landing down-wind, and there was a good deal blowing at the time. A few muttered and well-chosen imprecations from the Major were the only audible remarks from the audience. The machine (although the engine had been switched off) had a good deal of speed, and with the assistance of the wind flew straight through a distant hangar, to the surprise and disgust of a couple of mechanics who were talking scandal within. The hangar was a canvas one, but unfortunately there was a brick wall on the other side, and the remnants that were picked up were about two baskets full.

Another story with a moral, which also has its element of humour, is that of another great man who realising that flying is the simplest means of travel (if one can fly), and having to proceed to a large aerodrome some miles off to keep an engagement, thought that he would borrow a machine—not having one of his own handy. Owing to his exalted position he succeeded in achieving his ambition, and having had the fundamental principles explained to him he started off. Two hours later the temporary owner of the machine, having had no news of the arrival of the great man, telephoned to the aerodrome. "Well," was the answer, "a machine was piled up on the aerodrome about half an hour ago, and a staff officer stepped out of the debris—is that your man?"

It was. The great man now keeps his engagements in a well-appointed limousine.

CHAPTER 13

Salvage

"Hullo—Hullo—yes—who is it?"

The major reached for a pencil and listened to the faint sighs and moans down the wire. A ghostly voice started speaking. "Hullo. Is that you, Major? Well, No. 635 of your Squadron is down at Ack 2.5. Yes, near Dickebush lake—yes—crashed badly, pilot killed—will you send up there—right—I say, who was the pilot?"

The major opened a book and ran his finger down the machines "up"—he came to No. 635 and stopped. For a moment he looked out of the window with unseeing and tired eyes, then turned wearily to the telephone, "Hullo—it's Jimmy I'm afraid."

The wing adjutant at the other end of the wire frowned. "Oh, I'm damn sorry." He had been dining with the squadron the night before, and it was hard to realise that the dark curly-headed boy who had played the piano and sung and kept them laughing well into the night was dead. He sighed, and turned again to the pile of papers which grew momentarily on his desk.

The major sat for a moment at his table and stared at the book. "No. 635, 2nd Lieut. James———Patrol—left 5.45." He stared at the last gap, "returned"; which would never be filled in. "Oh, my God!" He got up, and hastily pushing a map into his pocket strode out to the transport shed; on the way he met the senior flight commander.

"Is everyone back, Jeffrey?"

"Yes, sir; all except 635,"

The major stopped and looked away over the aerodrome. "635 has crashed."

Jeffrey looked anxious. "Jimmy isn't hurt, is he, sir?"

"I'm afraid he's killed. I'm just going up there. Will you carry on."

The flight commander saluted and turned slowly away. Three-quarters of an hour later the car drew up at the foot of a small hill by a shattered house. All around the guns were roaring and stabbing the twilight with great flashes of yellow light. The major got out and entered a small cottage—one of the three that were more or less intact in the village. On the door was chalked "*Umpteen* Bde. Hqrs., Umpteen Division." He pushed the door open, and found a worried looking staff-captain wearing out pencils on masses of papers. He looked up when the major entered. "Oh, yes. Your machine is at the end of Tottenham Court Road in the front line trenches. Yes. It was shot down about an hour ago. They got the pilot out, but I'm afraid there's nothing left of the machine. You see it caught fire, and the Huns have been shelling for an hour what the fire left."

The major turned. "Thanks very much. I'll go up there. Can you let me have a guide?"

A small perspiring private was produced, and together they set off down through the mud and slush of the interminable trenches. Presently they came upon a large sign-board, which said in abrupt terms that Tottenham Court Road was to the left. By the board two officers were smoking. One of them turned when the major appeared. "Have you come after that machine, sir?"

"Well, we've sent back one of the guns and a few other things, and the body's here. Yes, he was shot, I think. Three Huns came at him out of a cloud, and I think some damned unlucky shot must have got him first go. He simply fluttered down like a leaf."

The major nodded and entered a dark little dug-out; on a form was a figure covered with a blanket.

He lifted one end and looked for a moment on the calm boyish face, with the curly dark hair round the forehead.

The major bent down, and lifting him up laid him tenderly on the stretcher.

An officer came up to him and placed a small package in his hand—the "articles of intrinsic value"—as the authorities have it—which would be sent to a heart-broken mother. Two mechanics entered and lifted the stretcher, and the major slowly led the way back to his car.

CHAPTER 14

Occasions

"And we had a most priceless occasion."

"Stop!" I said, pushing Jimmy into an armchair. "Ever since you returned from France your conversation has been rendered almost incoherent by strange words. Explain at once what you mean by an 'occasion'?" Jimmy smiled, lit a cigarette, and started off like this:—

There are times in the life of a pilot when flying becomes impossible on account of 'Dud' weather; there are times, I repeat, when melancholy creeps up and throws her arms about him, enveloping him in black despair. This may be due to many reasons; it may be indigestion; it may be the toot of a motor horn, conjuring up visions of Piccadilly seething with life and amusement, and that leave seems as far off as ever; or it may be the beginning of a cold in the head.

Anyway, he hates life with an enormous H, and makes himself a nuisance to everybody and a trial to himself. The sound of a cheery laugh acts like an incentive to murder. These are the times when an "occasion" is the only cure. It may strike someone well up in history that today is the anniversary of the battle of Waterloo; it may be somebody's birthday; it may be a full moon, or perhaps someone has been promoted (Jimmy stopped a moment and gazed fondly at six very new stars). One needn't look far to find a fairly substantial reason to mark the particular night with an occasion. Of course it isn't really necessary to have a reason at all; the mere fact that it's raining and cold, and that everyone is rather low is sufficient, but a reason always gives an added zest to the thing and a subject for the after-dinner speeches."

The procedure is as follow:—

First of all the O.C. drinks, and casts a knowing eye over his bottles. The result may be unsatisfactory. In this case he seizes the list of drink bills unpaid, and rushes round with a bloodshot look in his eye for the people whose instinct makes them disappear with miraculous quickness when they see the ominous figure approaching.

The Mess President, on being informed that an 'occasion' is necessary, proceeds to the kitchen with a much-soiled edition of *Mrs. Beeton* under his arm.

He probably suggests a very *récherché* dinner, while the cook, with the smile of the experienced, stands mute and horribly inglorious by his side. As he goes out of the kitchen he will probably hear subdued laughter and the words, 'Machonachie—tinned pears.' On the other hand, if the cook has half a drop of French blood in his veins, he will very likely produce a very good imitation of the *récherché* dinner ordered by the P.M.C. But cooks vary so much.

Half an hour before mess the ante-room would be filled with people agog with anticipation; in a corner of the room a man with upturned sleeves would be juggling with a great many bottles, finally finishing by performing an acrobatic feat with a cocktail shaker, while a crowd of people stand round him breathless with admiration and expectation. Five minutes before mess is announced, the ante-room buzzes with frivolous conversation and merry laughter, and the most trivial incident assumes quite a humorous aspect.

When the meal is over, the port passed round and the cigarettes alight, the major pushes back his chair and rises. If the major is very popular the cheering and rattle of knives, clapping of hands and stamping of feet goes on for quite a long time. In his speech he probably touches on some of the doings of the squadron, and if someone has been promoted, makes the usual congratulatory remarks, and proposes the toast. The remainder of the squadron then rise, drink the toast, and make the object of the toast thoroughly uncomfortable by telling him in song that he is a jolly good fellow. The remainder of the evening is passed in song and dance.

Possibly at an early hour someone happens to get outside; the sky is clear and ablaze with a thousand stars, and in the East Very lights pop up and fade slowly away. It's not unlikely that this same person has *not* to get up for an early shoot. He will then return to the mess with a big smile, and impart his disquieting news to those who *have* to get up early, and he will have to be agile if he escapes the shower of missiles which follow him out of the door. However, even such news as this, although it probably brings the squadron outside to gaze up at the stars and calculate the direction of the wind and the possibilities of the clouds, fails to stop the chuckles of the most pessimistic aviator. Finally, at an early hour, the squadron part and go chuckling and laughing to their respective huts. It requires so little to make one laugh after an 'occasion.'

Jimmy stopped and gazed thoughtfully at the blue spirals of smoke curling up from the cigarette.

CHAPTER 15

Lost

It was about twelve o'clock, and the day had been one of those annoying ones that fortunately don't come very often.

There are three distinct types of day to the aviator in war-time—a fine flying day, when the air is fine and crisp, the sky blue, and just a faint misty haze to upset Archie; the next type is the Dud day, when the sky is grey with dark, thick, hanging rain clouds, and you can scarcely see across the aerodrome; the last type is the day which is neither the one nor the other, great banks of misty clouds come racing across the sky, loose their shower of rain and scurry on, the sun struggles out, the sky gets blue, and then just as one is settled in the machine great bleak clouds and mist come racing up, obscuring everything with a heavy, drenching shower, and you get wearily out, crawl back to the mess hut and wait for the next gap in the clouds.

It was one of these last days that tinged Morelux's hair with white— at least Morelux said so. Most of the squadron had been engaged all the morning in the absorbing task of ousting rats, with the aid of Very lights and a small brown dog, from beneath the mess hut.

Archant, the squadron lunatic, was just giving his world-famed imitation of Buffalo Bill stalking a buffalo (the much harried rat in this instance was unconsciously the buffalo), when the inevitable orderly appeared.

"Mr. Morelux, sir, you're wanted at the office." The rat hunt continued, and Morelux, with a glance at the sky, hurried along to the office.

In the office he found the major, his flight commander, and his observer. The major turned as he came in. "Oh, Morelux, I think you might try Ack 1; it's a good target, and only just over the trenches. Good God, what's that? "The major stopped, outside the voices of many people, raised in triumph, got louder and louder. First of all a rat, dishevelled, and in the last stage of exhaustion staggered past the window, the wild look of the hunted in his eye. Then came a small brown mongrel, yelping and screaming, and a few yards behind come the squadron lunatic in an enormous pair of thigh boots, a dirty tunic, in one hand a light and in the other a large stick, shouting incoherent words of encouragement to anybody who came in sight. Then in various strange costumes, all shouting frantically, the rest of the squadron swept by.

The major turned with a smile. "Well, will you push up as soon as you can, Morelux? I've warned the battery." Morelux saluted, and turned to his observer. "Got the photo, Stilter?"

Stilter, always slow, but always accurate, smiled slowly and nodded.

Outside they met Archant exhausted, but triumphant. "Going up, Morelux?"

Morelux nodded and glanced up at the sky, which was getting clearer overhead, but darkening in the West.

Archant pulled out a noisily-coloured handkerchief and burst into theatrical tears—"Good-bye-e!"—and held out a trembling hand. Morelux laughed shortly, and arm-in-arm with his observer walked quickly over to "A" flight sheds, where his machine was waiting for him, with its three grimy satellites standing round it.

Ten minutes later, "Artillery, sir?" Stilter nodded languidly to the mechanic.

"Contact, sir?" queried the mechanic at the prop.

"Contact!" echoed Morelux. A twist of the prop., and a roar that became almost deafening died down as Morelux tested his revolutions and throttled down. A wave of the hand—the mechanic pulled away the chocks from under the wheel, and lifted the tail round until the machine was heading up-wind; then with an increasing roar the machine gradually started off and leaped over the grass—a couple of slight bumps and they were off the ground, five feet, ten, forty, up and up they soared, until after a couple of circuits round the aerodrome they had reached five hundred feet. Stilter glanced casually down and let out his aerial.

At eight thousand they had left the bumps far away below, and a few misty clouds raced away below them; in front of them, like some gigantic pock-marked morass, lay the salient and—Archie! To their left, far away, lay the grey sea, a thin white line marking the shore— and behind them great black clouds were banking up in large formi-

50

dable rolls.

In another ten minutes they were engrossed in their job. Stilter, with one gloved hand on the wireless key, his languid attitude gone, was peering over the side absorbed in his "shoot."

Morelux's time was divided between his instruments and rapid glances round the sky for enemy aircraft.

An hour went by. Suddenly Stilter, happening to glance round, was alarmed to see the great banks of thunder clouds coming up quickly behind them. He leant forward and touched Morelux's shoulder. Morelux looked round and took in the situation at a glance, and pointed downwards. Stilter nodded, and started to tap vigorously on the wireless key with one hand and wind up his aerial with the other.

Suddenly, without any warning, they were surrounded by the clouds, by a damp dark mist. Morelux pushed the joy stick forward and watched his altimeter—down, down, the air whistling and screaming through the wires—still clouds—clouds. Down again they went, their nose pointing towards home and safety. Suddenly the ground appeared dark and foreboding beneath them. Stilter glanced over the pilot's shoulder at the altimeter—three thousand feet, then he looked down. Beneath them lay a mass of water. Morelux shut off the engine, and turning round shouted, "Where are we?" Stilter craned his neck about.

"Over the floods," he shouted back, "but I'm not quite sure whereabouts."

Again he craned over the side—here and there a shattered home, roofless and desolate, stood out of the water.

Stilter glanced at the compass and noted they were going East. He waved to Morelux, and they turned round and flew straight for some minutes. Again he looked at the compass, and his heart for a second gave a flutter—it was still pointing East. Morelux turned round and made faces. "It's stuck," he shouted.

Stilter nodded and leant over the side. Everything was wrong. He looked for the wood and the town and the canal, popular landmarks, landmarks that on a fine day one could see for miles.

Everything seemed changed. He looked at his map, turned it every way, but failed to locate any spot. Added to their already uncomfortable position, the mist was growing thicker. They could only see directly beneath them now. Stilter looked frantically round and breathed a prayer. Morelux turned round and shook his head. Stilter smiled cheerily and looked down again hopelessly. Presently he waved down. Far away he had spotted a crowd of little white demolished houses.

Eagerly he clung to the frail hope that it might be Y——, although it looked hopelessly unfamiliar. They dropped two thousand feet in a dive towards it, but as they got over the town four loud cracks from Archie just behind the machine disillusioned them, and they again dived off at right angles. A slight rain had started, and the drops cut against their goggles and windscreen, making the visibility almost impossible. Below the trenches had vanished, and a dismal, unfriendly looking country was spread out beneath them.

Stilter threw his maps on the floor, and began to wonder if life in a prison camp was as bad as it was pictured; then he thought of the fire in the ante-room, and wondered who would have his hut. Suddenly the engine started spluttering. He saw Morelux bend forward; that was the last straw. Morelux switched off, and turning round beamed at Stilter and pointed down. Not two thousand feet below lay a long straight canal.

Stilter suddenly laughed loudly, and then suddenly felt rather like crying; he seized his map. "Thank God—there's Y——"; and signalling to Morelux to switch on again, he hurriedly located their position.

Why on earth didn't Morelux switch on? They were dropping quickly, and were only about two thousand feet up now. He looked up. Morelux pointed to the petrol-gauge. It was empty. "Can we do it?" yelled Stilter. Morelux nodded dubiously. Fifteen hundred feet—a thousand—seven hundred. They were dropping rapidly. At last the aerodrome appeared out of the gloom; five hundred feet, two hundred—it seemed as if they were just brushing the tree tops. At last they were over the aerodrome, a couple of bumps and they were on solid ground surrounded by mechanics.

They crawled out and, stretching themselves, walked over to the office. "Where the hell have you been?" said the major.

"Oh, we got a bit lost over the floods, sir," said Morelux.

"Shoot any good?"

"I think so, sir; we knocked out one gun position and put the wind up the rest," said Stilter.

"Good enough, run along and get some tea." The door closed, and the major stood for a moment looking out of the window. Then he opened a box, took out a cigarette, lit it thoughtfully, and his face wore a look of relief .

Liaison

In the ancient town of H—— is a market square; in the corner is a small shop; in the shop one may purchase the most exquisite chocolates. In the shop also is Juliette. When you first go into the shop you go to buy chocolates. Afterwards you very often go in just to see Juliette.

Sometimes when the War is far away, and the roll of London traffic fills the air, one meets a fellow-pilot who may have joined your squadron after you left it, or who patronized a neighbouring one, and your thoughts become reminiscent. "Do you remember H——?"

"Rather!"

"Do you remember that priceless little *estaminet*?"

"Oh, yes—the Lion d'Or."

"Yes, and did you ever meet Juliette?"

In every French town one remembers a Juliette—a dark-haired girl, slim and smiling, with dancing dark eyes and long lashes—always laughing, always gay—ready to teach French or to be taught English. She never laughed at one's appalling French, and her lisping English made conversation very agreeable. "Shall we visit the haunts of vice?" said Archant to Bobby one winter day. Bobby gazed at the heavy snow clouds hanging low in the sky and nodded. They dressed in all the finery of a clean tunic and a clean pair of boots, and having obtained leave set out upon the road to H——, a short mile away, with the happy feeling that the war was over for them till tomorrow morning.

"First of all," said Archant, "I must buy some shaving soap, and here is the very shop we want." Bobby gazed dubiously at the groceries displayed in the window and followed Archant.

"Leave the door open," said Archant with an experienced air. Bobby wondering left the door open, but once inside ceased to wonder, and gasped, "By Jove, Archant, give me a cigarette." An old lady appeared behind the counter looking remarkably healthy considering the closeness of the atmosphere, her hands full of knitting implements and wool.

"*Bon jour, M'sieurs.*"

"Good afternoon," said Archant. "Have you any shaving soap?" The old lady smiled pleasantly and inclined her head.

"*Pardon, M'sieur.*"

Archant gazed round the shop, but found no assistance. "*Avez- vous, de— de—*What is it, Bobby?"

Bobby chuckled, "Rub your chin."

"Oh, yes—*Madame—chose pour* shaving." An enlightened look passed over the old lady's face. She waddled to the window and presently produced a deadly-looking razor with a happy smile. Archant shook his head sadly and began to simulate a barber lathering Bobby.

"*Ah, oui, j'comprends.*" The old lady produced a shaving brush and a stick of soap. Archant seized upon the soap. They left the old lady smiling happily, and arrived at the Square.

"It's your turn to buy something now," said Archant.

Bobby looked nervous and pointed to a small shop in the corner. "Let's get some chocolates." They crossed over to the shop and went in. There was a peculiar absence of that aging element known as "fug," and as they looked at each other with questioning eyebrows a small door opened and a girl smiled behind the counter.

"*Bon jour, M'sieur.*" Bobby's pink face took a slightly deeper shade.

"*Bon jour,*" said Archant and started to discuss the prices and species of chocolates in a language which was more English than French Juliette neither winced nor smiled at hearing her language distorted almost beyond recognition.

"*Monsieur parle bien,*" she said quietly. Bobby drew his breath in sharply.

"I thought," he said, "it was my turn to buy something!" Half an hour later they were having tea in the Lion d'Or.

"Not a bad girl," said Archant.

"Not bad," said Bobby, "got rather a big mouth."

"Yes, and I didn't care much for the way she did her hair," said Archant.

"No," said Bobby.

★★★★★★

"Come in," said the major.

Bobby entered the office and saluted. "Is there anything for me to do, sir, this afternoon?"

The major looked at the rain pattering on the window and shook his head.

"Could I go to H——. I've got several things I want to buy."

"All right," said the major.

Bobby felt excited when he reached the Square at H——. He paused in front of a small chocolate shop and lit a cigarette. He noticed casually that there was an officer inside. Bobby took a long time to light the cigarette. He did it very carefully, and by the time he had put his matches away and buttoned up his coat again the officer had left.

"*Ah, bon jour. Monsieur Aviateur; votre ami ne viént pas c'après midi?*" Juliette raised her pretty eyebrows and smiled.

"No!" said Bobby, "he couldn't come this afternoon—he was busy." It was at that moment that the lie was punished. The door opened, a bell tinkled, and Archant walked in. Bobby said an extremely unpleasant word under his breath.

CHAPTER 17

"Bangers"

The flares on the aerodrome lit up the dim forms round them with a flickering light. McGuy looked up at the starlit sky and buttoned up his coat collar. "Hell of a game," he murmured, and thought of the stove in his hut, and Bobby lying an inert lump in bed. A far away clock struck eleven as McGuy climbed into his machine. The engine suddenly roared and softened down. The machine taxied out towards the flares and turned into the wind. Again the engine roared, and the machine leapt forward and rose into the air. When distance had softened the roar of the engine to a gentle murmur, a bored mechanic yawned and turned towards the sheds, taking the whole thing as a matter of course. McGuy, from a height of two thousand feet, looked up at the cold twinkling stars, and down again at the tiny points of fire—the flares on the aerodrome.

For ten more minutes he climbed, and then turned towards the East. Far away behind him a dim searchlight moved in a white line about the sky. A tiny electric bulb lit up his instruments and map. McGuy yawned and began to hum to himself. There was nothing but black all around him now. Even the pale light of the stars had been obscured by fleecy clouds. Far below tiny Very lights faded above the trenches.

McGuy glanced at his map and slightly altered his direction. His feet were getting cold and he stamped them on the floor. Presently he glanced again at his map and down at a few misty lights clustering in front far below. His heart beat slightly faster as he shut off his engine and started to spiral down.

The whistling wires sounded very soft after the even roar of the engine. Suddenly a great pencil of white light shot up from the ground and formed a white circle on the clouds above him. Two more on either side leapt up and began to wave from side to side. McGuy turned and dived, and the whistle of the wires rose to a scream. Suddenly one of the great beams of light caught him, and for a moment dazzled him. "Damn and blast!" he murmured as he turned and twisted, but the beam held him, and the two others raced across the sky to add to his discomfiture. Four balls of flame burst away on his right with sharp "crumps." Again he dived and twisted, and suddenly found himself in the dark. He glanced at his altimeter; the tiny luminous needle pointed to 500.

For a moment he glanced anxiously below, wishing he had the advantage of a cat's eyes, and then released a bomb. A few seconds of suspense, and a tiny flame burst up from the ground, revealing for a moment a few trees and a house and a sparkle of water. McGuy swore loudly and dived. The searchlights were waving excitedly round the sky, groping with their long white arms to find him.

At two hundred feet he flattened out. A watery moon had risen and by its dim light, with a sigh of relief, he caught sight of his landmark. Again he released a bomb and watched. By the glare of the explosion he saw a large building and a few dim houses around it. Quickly he released the remainder and started to climb. A huge red glare flickered round his machine, and looking down he saw great red flames and rosy clouds of smoke curling up; tiny figures surged down the narrow roads. Turning towards the west he climbed as fast as he could.

Again the machine was lit up in a blinding glare of white light, and again McGuy swore loudly. Shells began to burst above him and in front of him. The sky in front seemed to be alive with great red flashes. Twisting and turning he tried to avoid them. The remorseless fight held him, and a sudden deafening crash made the machine shiver and tremble like a frightened animal. "All right—damn you!" he murmured, and turning dived at the great white eye beneath. The cold wind raced against his face and screamed around. He pressed the trigger of the gun, and the eye winked for a moment at him and disappeared. Again he turned and faced the bursting shells. Far away beyond he saw a dim friendly searchlight groping round the stars. A sudden blinding flash in front made his heart leap, and the acrid smell of powder, as he flew through the smoke of the shell, made him wrinkle his nose.

With a sigh of relief he saw a Very light pop up below him, and a moment later the tiny flames on the aerodrome flickered and beckoned to him. He switched off and spiralled down. The lights grew larger and larger, and a moment later he was skimming between them.

"Any luck?" said the major, as McGuy entered the office blowing on his fingers. McGuy tried to conceal an intensely satisfied feeling behind a bored expression.

"Yes, sir, I think I got it."

"Good enough," said the major, and turned towards the telephone.

CHAPTER 18

The Vacant Seat

When one first goes out to France leave is so remote that one doesn't think about it, but as time goes on, senior people start to go and one finds oneself looking more often at the leave roaster. Cautious remarks creep into letters, and in the peace and silence of one's bed, leave assumes a more concrete aspect. Though still dim and distant, plans begin to formulate, and very likely the bank pass book arrives and calculations follow.

On the Friday of the particular week I'm thinking about, Jimmy had just finished giving the major his report after a long and trying patrol when the telephone rang. The major listened, smiled, and looked at the leave roaster. Jimmy's eyes followed the major's, and with a slight thumping in the left side of his breast realized that the next to go on leave was himself.

"Right," said the major down the telephone. "Lieut. James—good-bye-e-e." Jimmy tried to look nonchalant. The major turned. "There's a seat going tomorrow, Jimmy." Jimmy smiled, thanked the major, saluted and hurried away. Leave had at last become a reality.

The first thing he did was to write two letters. They were brief and contained the plans which for weeks he had been formulating, but had not dared to actually write.

The next thing he did was to arrange an "occasion," to cheer up the people who weren't going on leave.

The following morning he awoke with a feeling of impending pleasure—and realizing quickly the full significance of the feeling, dressed himself rapidly, packed slowly, dwelling happily on every article he put in his suit case and for the remainder of the morning made himself a general nuisance on the aerodrome, pointing out to pilots who were just going "up" the extraordinary prevalence of "Archie" and imaginary "Huns."

"I think we're going to have a spell of fine weather now," he persisted in remarking to anyone who would listen to him.

Twelve o'clock and the tender arrived, and Jimmy emerged from his hut as spotless as his servant, who had laboured for two hours the night before, could make him.

His face was shining and was wreathed in smiles, and his pockets bulged with a dozen written injunctions from the other less fortunate pilots whose wardrobe or cigarette cases required replenishing.

Followed by half-a-dozen "good-bye-e-e's" the tender moved off, and Jimmy sank back and puffed at his cigarette with a feeling of perfect and absolute content.

There are few men, now, that have not experienced that feeling, which no words can describe, of standing on the deck and watching the cliffs of England grow nearer and larger.

England!—after five months of war. Jimmy found himself talking to strange people as if he had known them all his life. Already France was in the dim past. Was it only twenty-four hours or a week ago that he had left the aerodrome and the ominous sounds of distant Archie guns.

With an ear-splitting roar the siren called to the harbour. The boat slipped alongside the quay and Jimmy, with a bag clasped in his right hand and a stick in the left, found himself in the tide of happy people, being borne over the gangway and down towards the train.

There were many things he noticed with subconscious pleasure. Boys were shouting in Cockney English, there was an air of method and cleanliness about the Pullman Car, English papers were pushed under his nose, and the English air smelt wonderfully sweet and fresh. Jimmy pressed his nose against the window, and watched the green fields and hedges racing by. The speed of the train after the agonizing crawl of the French train sent a thrill through him.

The fields changed to houses. With a rumble they crossed the Thames and five minutes later slowed up alongside the platform. With a bang Jimmy wrenched the door open and sprang out. For a moment he glanced round hesitatingly, and then he caught sight of two ladies —one elderly and the other one young; both were smiling with curious lights in their eyes. Jimmy advanced. The war was forgotten.

Fritz

"Hullo," said someone, "there's a Hun." All eyes were at once turned up in the direction of the pointed finger, and the air was filled with experienced surmises as to the species. Far above the small white speck pursued its course with absolute indifference to the small white clustering puffs from the anti-aircraft guns, and after circling once or twice over the aerodrome slowly drifted out of sight. It was so unusual a sight for a Hun to appear alone in the full daylight six miles over the line, that as a topic of conversation it lasted for quite a long while. "I bet we're bombed tonight," said the squadron pessimist. "I expect some of his pals dared him to do it, or he did it for a bet."

The War Baby smiled. "It must have been a hell of a bet to make him come right over here!"

No bombs disturbed their sleep that night, but next morning the Hun appeared at the same time flying over the same course.

It looked so fat and lazy and insolent, as it quietly hummed high above the drifting clouds, that the major frowned and retired into the office with the senior flight commander. Presently the flight commander reappeared, smiling. Nine o'clock the following morning a large German, expensively clad in furs, walked slowly across an aerodrome six miles over the wrong side of the line.

His breakfast had been a good one, but his mind seemed to be uneasy and he frowned as he walked. By the sheds a large machine was gently swaying to the breeze. "Our final trip," he grunted to the sergeant pilot. The pilot sprung to attention with an expressionless face.

A few minutes later they were roaring up into the wind, and the fur-clad figure in the back seat gazed dubiously towards the West. It wasn't until the altimeter registered twelve thousand feet that they left the aerodrome and headed towards the trenches. The observer gazed languidly round the empty skies, and settled himself more comfortably in his seat.

As they passed over the trenches a few shells started to burst with sudden crumps behind them. The German smiled. "So bad, they've given it up," he murmured, as the bursts got further away and eventually stopped. A few minutes later he was leaning over the side, peering down at the little line of sheds at the edge of an aerodrome, his hand resting lovingly on the bomb release. He noted with satisfaction that a line of machines lay close together outside the hangars.

Directed by a wave of his hand to the pilot the machine swung gently round, and he was about to release his bombs when an uncanny feeling made him glance round over his shoulder; he dropped the bomb release and seized his gun. Not fifty yards behind a machine was flying slightly above them. As he seized his gun a stream of flashing bullets cracked past his head. Cursing at the top of his voice, he signalled rapidly to the pilot. In a second the machine tilted down and flashed away in a vertical nose dive. Two thousand feet below the pilot pulled it out, and the observer gazed round with terrified eyes.

There above them at the same distance was the tiny scout. The bullets started again to crack round him; he caught hold of his gun and pulled the trigger, firing wildly in circles round the machine above him. A sudden jar on his elbow and a numbing pain down his right arm made him drop the gun with a curse. A hopeless feeling of terror obsessed his mind, and he turned and shrieked at the pilot, "Dive! Get away from the devil for the love of God!" A bullet tore a burning line across his cheek. He turned again, and as he looked a flame burst from the front of his machine and leapt towards him along the fabric.

White-faced and shivering he watched the pilot struggling with the little tube of fire extinguisher. The smouldering fabric burst into flame, and furiously he tried to beat it out with his gloves, but in a second the fire was all round him. Dimly he heard the pilot screaming through the cloud of smoke. They were flashing down in a wild uncontrolled dive. The wind screamed around him; the flames leapt about his leather coat and tore the skin from his face with burning fingers.

★★★★★★

Two hundred feet above a little scout flew around in circles. The pilot was gazing down at the black smoking patch in the centre of a ploughed field below.

CHAPTER 20

Mr. Meteor

I know few people so persistently optimistic as Mr. Meteor. Although I have never met him, I have frequently thought of him as a little short fellow with a high brow, wrinkled by concentration, sitting on his lawn surrounded by his favourite instruments. The day is a summer one and the heat shimmers up from the ground, making one long for the sound and touch of cool, clear water. Mr. Meteor sits with a large white handkerchief over his head, watching the clouds. "Poor lads," he murmurs sympathetically from time to time.

Amongst the mass of important envelopes on the major's desk, lies a modest little note, the weather report for tomorrow. It portends rain, and breezes from the north; the sky will be partly covered by clouds—the temperature is going down.

The major sitting in the hot little office, his coat off and shirt sleeves rolled up, his forehead damp with perspiration, feels stronger. The vision of the fresh glittering raindrops and cool cloud shadows fill him with thankfulness. "Ah," he says to Jewsker Broske, the gaunt Australian flight commander, "thank God, the weather is going to change."

"I hope it won't get too cold to bathe," says Broske.

The morrow dawns, a cloudless sky, the sun rises and starts to burn. "I expect the clouds will be coming up soon," says Broske; "fine before seven rain at eleven, you know." At eleven the sky is still an unbroken sketch of blue, and the sun burns more than ever. The major glances at Mr. Meteor's note a little dubiously.

The sun subsides in a blaze of red and ends one of the warmest days of the year.

But no one can be angry with Mr. Meteor, he always means so well.

On one occasion he certainly was a little bit trying. It was during a spell of dud weather, when the mist and heavy clouds made aerial war an impossibility.

For two days we had been idling and polishing our French in the neighbouring towns, happy days they were. On the third day the major found a little note from Mr. Meteor:—"Visibility tomorrow will be good, clouds nil, temperature rising, wind moderate." The Major at once detailed the machines and we all stood by. We stood by for three days before we realized that Mr. Meteor was merely perpetrating another of his little jokes upon us, and who can say, now we understand him, how much we would miss that happy little optimistic note from Mr. Meteor if for one day it failed to turn up. Who can say? I can't!

CHAPTER 21

Side Shows

It came through in the late afternoon of a grilling summer's day. We were idling in towels on the bank of the canal, watching the stream move slowly down with its burden of defunct animals. (It took more than a week-dead cat to stop one plunging into the cool water during those hot summer days, when the simple effort of walking assumed the proportions of violent exercise and made one's clothes wet with perspiration.)

Jimmy was nonchalantly throwing stones at a piece of flotsam which might have once been a dog, when a panting orderly arrived. "All officers wanted at the office, sir!" We dressed rapidly with the feeling of "coming events," and walked quickly to the office. The CO. in his shirt sleeves was sucking a pencil, and before him on the table lay large maps. We gathered round him and listened intently. That night we talked in measured tones about the show that was coming, observers and pilots closeted themselves together with maps, paste, and three-ply, and argued about which would search the ground and which would distend his eyeballs up into the skies in search of cross-marked enemies.

The mechanical maniac doubled his output of gadgets and spent most of the night in the workshop lorry, fiddling with wires and wheels. Very early the next morning a dull roll of guns started, punctuated every few minutes by thudding explosions.

On the aerodrome, in the dawn-mist, dim figures pulled the machines out, and muffled figures climbed into them. The engines roared and softened down as they taxied out on to the aerodrome. One by one they roared up into the air. Billy, sitting with fur up to his eyes, felt that "early morning" feeling acutely and looked down rather enviously at the huts below, where several happy aviators, whose jobs started at ten o'clock, still slept profoundly. "How I should love to know," murmurs the fond mother, "what the brave lad's thoughts were about!"

The brave lad's thoughts were probably more or less after this fashion: "Wish to God I'd shoved on that extra pair of socks." "Where the hell did I put that pencil?" "Lucky fellows those Inland Water Transport." "What the hell do they want to send us up so damned early for? Shan't see a thing." "Might have easily had another hour in bed without spoiling the war." "Funny-shaped head old Nimrod's got" (the pilot in front). "Wonder where he gets his flying cap from." "By Jove, look at that." Billy, craning over the side, saw long lines of shells bursting without cessation about the trenches in a sea of small white puffs. From time to time a red tongue of flame would shoot up and give way to a roll of black smoke.

The stars had quite gone, and the pale sun drove away the light curtain of mist. Archie started and crumped vigorously behind them. The sky was full of machines above and below—large single ones, intent on their shoots, swift small ones darting like dragon flies, escorting clusters of large bombing formations droning eastwards with their load of bombs, while around them all was a halo of black smudgy Archie. Far below were the little contact patrol machines zigzagging along engaged in their hazardous task of supplying Headquarters with a constant stream of information in the form of messages clothed in gaudy streamers. Behind them lay a silent row of observation balloons.

Billy looked at his watch and glanced down—the barrage was lifting and moving forward. A line of squat black things were moving after it. Billy's lips formed the word "Tanks" as he patted his pilot's head and pointed down.

The pilot nodded and, looking down, waggled his joy-stick in appreciation of the extraordinary scene. Billy scanned the skies, with a finger on his gun—once or twice a machine started to dive on them, but quickly turned when it spotted their rings.

When they had finished their shoot, and had seen with satisfaction their target in flames, they dived down towards the trenches and home. For a time they watched the shells bursting in the apparently empty Hun trenches; then as the bumps from passing explosives and the rat-tat-tat of machine guns was becoming unhealthy, they climbed up again and turned towards the aerodrome and breakfast. It's not an unpleasant sensation after three and a-half hours in an atmosphere full of war and hate, to shut off the engine and glide quietly back to the aerodrome. The wind no longer shrieks at you as it rushes by, the quiet whistles of the propeller is very soothing after the roar of the engine, and the probability is that your job's over for the day, and you've got the pleasant anticipation of a good meal and about sixteen or seventeen hours' peace and happiness before the next errand to Hunland starts.

At breakfast the air was full of "Did you see the ——?"

"My engine was priceless; going like this"—little Morelux growled in an attempt to imitate the even roar of a well-running engine.

"Yes, I saw two batteries go up in flames."

"Gawd, only two? I saw five."

"See the Tanks; oh, priceless"—and so on. Every now and then another couple of oil-smudged aviators would enter, full of new incidents and casting happy eyes at the eggs and bacon.

By nine o'clock the aerodrome was deserted, every machine was in the air; a few mechanics, idle for the moment, gazed eastwards at the tiny dots flying about like angry bees, pursued by tiny balls of black. A Napoleonic figure in a black leather coat stood watching the distant scene through a pair of binoculars, longing to be "up" and sharing the excitement with his pilots. In many ways, "The major's" lot was a hard one; and he hated the telephone and the small voice that whispers, "One of your machines down at ——."

Towards evening the visibility began to get bad, and one by one the machines returned and the pilots, tired and dirty, crowded into the office to make their reports.

A dishevelled recording officer wrote feverishly in a large book. In every case the answer to "any enemy aircraft seen? "was "Nil," but everyone had a lot to say about their shoots!

At six o'clock the light was very bad; all the machines, except one, were down. Four or five pilots were out on the aerodrome, watching a black speck that was droning in from the east. "There he is," said someone.

"No, it isn't," said someone else.

"Yes, it is."

"No, it isn't," as the speck passed over the aerodrome and droned on away to the west. A few minutes later another speck appeared, and this time it grew larger, spiralled down, landed, and out jumped Billy and his pilot, rosy and oily.

Explanations followed. "Everyone down," said Billy.

"Everyone o.k.," said someone, and arm-in-arm they all wandered over to the mess to wash and change. Later on the news came through that the show had been a "walk over," so to speak; and at the same time came a polite message of congratulation on the squadron's efforts from a great man. There was *"beaucoup"* jubilation in the mess that night.

Ten Minutes

Extract from any Daily Paper:—

Two enemy machines were brought down in flames.

Extract from Official *Communique*:—

Lieut. Smith and Lieut. Jones, No. *Umpteen* Squadron, whilst on artillery observation were attacked by two E. A. scouts, one of which they shot down in flames, the other was last seen going down in a vertical nose dive.

"Contact," said Smith looking over his shoulder at Williams. Williams smiled and nodded, the engine roared and they taxied out into the wind; quickly they rose up into the air and droned away to the east. A few minutes later Williams was gazing round the blue and white sky and tapping pensively on the wireless key. Tiny figures far below pulled out white signals. He watched until they had finished, then he put his hand out, squeezed his pilot's shoulder and pointed towards the target which was a blue-blurred wood some miles over the line. Smith nodded and headed towards it.

A thin bank of mist a few hundred feet above them smudged the sky to a pale blue. They were over the target now, and as Williams was gazing down a sudden startling crack by his head made him leap round and seize his gun. He stared up into the blazing sun, a blurred black object was swooping down upon them—again the cracks started and their machine started to quiver. Quickly sighting his gun he pulled the trigger, cool fingered and steady, and followed the enemy machine as it dived; his gun suddenly stopped, and he cursed at the top of his voice. Smith was banking vertically, and he struggled to get his gun going again.

They were now on top of the Hun, who had finished his dive and was turning; their forward gun started as they dived on the twisting scout. Williams, out of one eye, saw the stream of flashing bullets pass right into the middle of the machine, but nothing seemed to happen. He got his gun going again, and as they dived past he fired into the scout from point blank range. With a feeling of wild excitement and elation he saw it side-slip and spin, while a great stream of black smoke and flame poured out of the fuselage.

Smith was leaning over the side watching, and Williams patted him on the back with a trembling gloved hand. Again Williams' heart suddenly leaped and raced, a feeling as if someone had brought a cane hard down an inch from his foot made him wheel round; he had a vision of a white machine with great black smudges on its wings diving at them from the left. "Gawd," he whispered, and hit his pilot and pointed. Almost simultaneously their machine banked vertically and stalling they faced the enemy. The forward gun again began to spit out fire—while bullets from the Hun splintered and cracked about their heads.

As the German machine flashed by them, Williams had an instant vision of a black, muffled figure crouching inside the black and white body, and then in a moment it had disappeared below them, and while Williams watched it came into view again, falling like a stone far away below until it vanished into the mist.

They were gliding quietly towards the hues, Williams lay back and wondered what his pilot's thoughts were about. With a soft whistle of the propeller they glided on to the aerodrome and bumped to a standstill.

Williams got out, and suddenly realised he was trembling. He got out a cigarette, and after a rapid inspection of their machine, which was full of holes and tears, they strode arm in arm to the office.

Two figures in oily leather coats and with dishevelled hair stood before the major in the office. "Do any good?" said the major.

Smith, the pilot, smiled. "I'm afraid we couldn't finish that shoot, sir, we were attacked by two E. A."

"No?" said the major, looking serious.

"Yes, sir,—Jones and I," said Smith, nodding his head at Jones, who was still quivering with excitement. "Jones and I had only just got over the target, when one of the dirty dogs dived on our tail, between the sun. We banked as hard as we could, and Jones loosed off with his gun."

"The damned gun jambed," broke in Jones breathlessly.

"He got it going again," continued Smith, "and the little blighter must have got him in the second burst, because he went down with gubbins and flame and stuff pouring out."

"Nonsense," said Jones, "it was your gun that got him—just after we turned."

"And then," said Smith, ignoring the interruption, "we were just watching him go down when a couple of bullets got my altimeter."

Jones, refusing to remain passive any longer, exploded with long pent-up emotions. "We got round again and I pooped off as hard as I could, but the gun stopped again and I couldn't clear it, but Smith got round and put a couple of good bursts into the Hun just as he was turning to climb. Nothing seemed to happen for a moment and I thought he'd missed, when suddenly the Hun side-slipped, spun, flattened out, and went down in a split-act dive. We couldn't see him crash, as he went into a bank of mist near the ground."

"Damn good!" said the major, beaming, as he turned towards the telephone.

CHAPTER 23

The Last Flight

It was a fairly fine day, and the ante-room was almost empty. Three people sprawled in unconventional attitudes in three armchairs—Archant, the squadron lunatic; Billy, the War Baby; and Ethelred, the Unready. Archant was fair, with tousled hair; Billy—well everyone knows the War Baby; and Ethelred was plump, always well-groomed, and always unready. Archant was absorbed in the English translation of a French novel; Ethelred was attempting to make a dishevelled fly loop the loop; and Billy was looking disconsolate and very bored. "*Take a pair of sparkling eyes*," sung Billy in uncertain tones.

"Go and take them outside," said Archant unfeelingly, and turned over a page.

"Ethelred, old Bean," said Billy, breaking the silence five minutes later, "what's your greatest worry?"

"Getting out of bed," answered the looping instructor promptly, as the fly, wearied unto death, dropped on to the floor. "What's yours?"

"I think," said Billy plaintively, "Archant is." Ethelred looked at Archant, remembered Billy was his observer, and nodded his head slowly.

"Yes, I don't wonder. Yes, I should hate to have a pilot like that—it looks so bad, doesn't it?"

"What the devil do you mean—you blistered son of a Hun?" said Archant loudly. Billy screamed and emulated a lady of fashion afflicted with the vapours. "Who was it that fired on one of his own machines, eh?" continued Archant, brutally referring to an old *contre-temps*.

Ethelred, taken unawares, groped for red hot words. Fortunately, an orderly entered and saluted at Archant. "Wanted in the office, sir."

Archant nodded "Right," and seizing his cap disappeared through the window.

Billy sniffed. "I have an ugly presentiment, Ethelred, that shortly I shall be compelled to aviate."

"Your presentiment," said Ethelred—safe with a cut hand—"is not without foundation. Archant is waving from the office. Go, my child, and *Allah* be with you."

Billy flung a magazine at Ethelred's sleek hair and walked out towards the office. Archant met him with outstretched hands. "Fly with me, little one?"

Billy grunted, "What have we got to do?"

"One little trench reconnaissance—is it too much I ask of you?"

Billy frowned, "Oh, dry up and let's see." Archant produced photographs and a sheet of paper on which several leading questions were type-written—first, an arrow pointing to a small pin-point on the photograph and the question, "Is this a cookhouse?"—another arrow pointing to a brown mess and the question "What is this?" and so on. They studied them at length. Twenty minutes later little Billy, enveloped in vast quantities of fur clothing, gazed inquisitively over the side of the machine at the trenches below. He was attempting from a height of 1,500 feet to discover if the pin-point on the photograph actually was a cookhouse, or if it was a machine gun emplacement covered in subtle camouflage.

From time to time Archant wrote messages on a writing block in front of him, which Billy, leaning over his shoulder, read with difficulty. "We'd better go down a bit." Billy nodded with an expressionless face, and as Archant switched off the engine they could faintly hear the tat-tat-tat of machine guns and the occasional crack of a well-aimed bullet by their speeding heads. They were far too low for Archie's groping burst, and Huns seldom ventured to such low altitudes over the trenches, so they had only Fritz's rifle and machine gun bullets to cope with. Billy watched the altimeter; the needle quivered round 1,500—1,000.

Archant switched on, and with a spluttering roar the engine burst into song again. Billy fixed his eyes on the trenches below, and tried to ignore the zip-zip of a couple of bullets that splintered the wood work, besides his arm. Down they roared until they could see the white upturned faces of the crouching figures in the trenches, and then with a shriek of wires Archant pulled her up, and they shot up again towards the West. After the fourth dive Billy had answered most of the required questions, but to make sure of the last he signalled to Archant to dive again. Archant frowned and looked at the rev-counter needle, which was quivering and dropping, but nodded his head and banked again. A whistling shriek of wires and they dived, with the engine spluttering badly—down, down, down—the wind screaming by their ears—and then suddenly Billy's heart and the engine ceased almost simultaneously—but Billy's heart went on with redoubled vigour.

Archant was calmly fiddling with something in front. They were two hundred feet now, and the bullets were ripping, splintering and tearing the fabric all round them. A wire broke with a metallic "ping," and Billy clenched his hands for a moment—then, thrusting his papers into his pockets, he seized his gun and pulling back the cocking handle pulled the trigger, spraying the crouching figures in the trenches with bursts of tracer bullets. Archant, the squadron lunatic, when the engine stopped, drew a sudden breath, and his hands tightened on the joy stick—a bullet splashed a score of splinters round his face and made him shake his head, and then he laughed as he caught sight of the switch—his elbow had knocked it up. "Jove, what a damned fool!" he whispered, and quickly pressed it down.

A hesitating splutter, and the engine burst into a tremulous roar. They were a hundred feet now, and had left the trenches away behind them. Billy had stopped firing, and with the engine going well Archant cast a quick look behind him. He saw Billy lying in a curiously pathetic heap. "Gad!" he whispered, and quickly looked for the nearest aerodrome. At last he caught sight of the hangars, and glided quickly down to a gentle standstill. Mechanics ran out as they arrived, and Archant turned round in his seat. Billy looked up plaintively—white-faced.

"I'm all right, old Bean! I caught one in the tummy I think," he gasped.

Carefully they lifted him out and put him on a stretcher. "In my pocket," he gasped painfully. Archant nodded, and putting his hand in Billy's pocket drew out the photographs and papers. "I—put—the—wind—up—the Huns," whispered Billy, and fainted.

Cavalry of the Clouds

"Contact"

Contents

DEDICATED
TO
THE FALLEN OF *UMPTY* SQUADRON, R.F.C.
JUNE–DECEMBER 1916

Preface

Of the part played by machines of war in this war of machinery the wider public has but a vague knowledge. Least of all does it study the specialised functions of army aircraft. Very many people show mild interest in the daily reports of so many German aeroplanes destroyed, so many driven down, so many of ours missing, and enraged interest in the reports of bomb raids on British towns; but of aerial observation, the main *raison d'etre* of flying at the front, they own to nebulous ideas.

As an extreme case of this haziness over matters aeronautic I will quote the lay question, asked often and in all seriousness: "Can an aeroplane stand still in the air?" Another surprising point of view is illustrated by the home-on-leave experience of a pilot belonging to my present squadron. His lunch companion—a charming lady—said she supposed he lived mostly on cold food while in France.

"Oh no," replied the pilot, "it's much the same as yours, only plainer and tougher."

"Then you do come down for meals," deduced the lady. Only those who have flown on active service can fully relish the comic savour of a surmise that the Flying Corps in France remain in the air all day amid all weathers, presumably picnicking, between flights, off sandwiches, cold chicken, pork pies, and mineral waters.

These be far-fetched examples, but they serve to emphasise a general misconception of the conditions under which the flying services carry out their work at the big war. I hope that this my book, written for the most part at odd moments during a few months of training in England, will suggest to civilian readers a rough impression of such conditions. To Flying Officers who honour me by comparing the descriptions with their own experiences, I offer apology for whatever they may regard as "hot air," while submitting in excuse that the narratives are founded on unexaggerated fact, as anyone who served with *Umpty* Squadron through the Battle of the Somme can bear witness.

I have expressed a hope that the chapters and letters will suggest a rough impression of work done by R.F.C. pilots and observers in France. A complete impression they could not suggest, any more than the work of a Brigade-Major could be regarded as representative of that of the General Staff. The Flying-Corps-in-the-Field is an organisation great in numbers and varied in functions. Many separate duties are allotted to it, and each separate squadron, according to its type of machine, confines itself to two or three of these tasks.

The book, then, deals only with the squadron to which I belonged last year, and it does not pretend to be descriptive of the Flying Corps as a whole. Ours was a crack squadron in its day, and, as General Brancker has mentioned in his Introduction, it held a melancholy record in the number of its losses. *Umpty's* Squadron's casualties during August, September, and October of 1916 still constitute a record for the casualties of any one flying squadron during any three months since the war began. Once eleven of our machines were posted as "missing" in the space of two days—another circumstance which has fortunately never yet been equalled in R.F.C. history. It was a squadron that possessed excellent pilots, excellent achievements, and the herewith testimonial in a letter found on a captured German airman, with reference to the machine of which we then had the Flying Corps monopoly: "The most-to-be-feared of British machines is the S——."

Our duties were long reconnaissance, offensive patrols around German air country, occasional escort for bombing craft, and occasional photography. I have but touched upon other branches of army aeronautics; though often, when we passed different types of machine, I would compare their job to ours and wonder if it were more pleasant. Thousands of feet below us, for example, were the artillery craft, which darted backward and forward across the lines as from their height of vantage they ranged and registered for the guns. On push days these same buses were to be seen lower still, well within range of machine-gun bullets from the ground, as they crawled and nosed over the line of advance and kept intelligent contact between far-ahead attacking infantry and the rear.

Above the tangled network of enemy defences roved the line photography machines, which provided the Staff with accurate survey maps of the Boche defences. Parties of bombers headed eastward, their lower wings laden with eggs for delivery at some factory, aerodrome, headquarter, railway junction, or ammunition dump. Dotted everywhere, singly or in formations of two, three, four, or six, were those aristocrats of the air, the single-seater fighting scouts. These were envied for their advantages. They were comparatively fast, they could turn, climb, and stunt better and quicker than any two-seater, and their petrol-tanks held barely enough for two hours, so that their shows were soon completed. All these varied craft had their separate functions, difficulties, and dangers. Two things only were shared by all of us—dodging Archie and striving to strafe the Air Hun.

Since those days flying conditions on the Western Front have been much changed by the whirligig of aeronautical development. All things considered, the flying officer is now given improved opportunities. Air fighting has grown more intense, but the machines in use are capable of much better performance. The latest word in single-seater scouts, which I am now flying, can reach 22,000 feet with ease; and it has a maximum climb greater by a third, and a level speed greater by a sixth, than our best scout of last year. The good old one-and-a-half strutter (a fine bus of its period), on which we used to drone our way around the 150-mile reconnaissance, has disappeared from active service. The nerve-edging job of long reconnaissance is now done by more modern two-seaters, high-powered, fast, and reliable, which can put up a fight on equal terms with anything they are likely to meet. The much-discussed B.E., after a three-year innings, has been replaced for the most part by a better-defended and more satisfactory artillery bus. The F.E. and de Haviland pushers have likewise become obsolete. The scouts which we thought invincible last autumn are badly outclassed by later types.

For the rest, the Flying Corps in France has grown enormously in size and importance. The amount of work credited to each branch of it has nearly doubled during the past year—reconnaissance, artillery observation, photography, bombing, contact patrol, and, above all, fighting. Air scraps have tended more and more to become battles between large formations. But most significant is the rapid increase in attacks by low-flying aeroplanes on ground personnel and materiel, a branch which is certain to become an important factor in the winning of the war.

And this whirlwind growth will continue. The world at large, as distinct from the small world of aeronautics, does not realize that aircraft will soon become predominant as a means of war, any more than it reckons with the subsequent era of universal flight, when designers, freed from the subordination of all factors to war requirements, will give birth to machines safe as motor-cars or ships, and capable of carrying heavy freights for long distances cheaply and quickly. Speaking of an average pilot and a non-expert enthusiast, I do not believe that even our organisers of victory are yet aware of the tremendous part which aircraft can be made to take in the necessary humbling of Germany.

Without taking into account the limitless reserve of American aerial potentiality, it is clear that within a year the Allies will have at their disposal many thousands of war aeroplanes. A proper apportionment of such of them as can be spared for offensive purposes could secure illimitable results. If for no other cause it would shorten the war by its effect on civilian nerves. We remember the hysterical outburst of rage occasioned by the losses consequent upon a daylight raid on London of some fifteen machines, though the public had become inured to the million military casualties since 1914. What, then, would be the effect on German war-weariness if giant raids on fortified towns by a hundred or so allied machines were of weekly occurrence? And what would be the effect on our own public if giant raids on British towns were of weekly occurrence? Let us make the most of our aerial chances, and so forestall betrayal by war-weariness, civilian pacifism, self-centred fools, and strange people.

From an army point of view the probable outcome of an extensive aerial offensive would be still greater. Well-organised bomb raids on German aerodromes during the night and early morning have several times kept the sky clear of hostile aircraft during the day of an important advance. If this be achieved with our present limited number of bombing machines, much more will be possible when we have double or treble the supply. Imagine the condition of a particular sector of the advanced lines of communication if it were bombed every day by scores of aeroplanes. Scarcely any movement would be possible until bad weather made the attacks non-continuous; and few supply *depôts* in the chosen area would afterwards remain serviceable. Infantry and artillery dependent upon this district of approach from the rear would thus be deprived of essential supplies.

Apart from extensive bombing, an air offensive of at least equal value may happen in the form of machine-gun attacks from above. Today nothing seems to panic the Boche more than a sudden swoop by a low-flying aeroplane, generous of bullets, as those of us who have tried this game have noticed. No German trench, no emplacement, no battery position, no line of transport is safe from the R.F.C. Vickers and Lewis guns; and retaliation is difficult because of the speed and erratic movement of the attacking aeroplane. Little imagination is necessary to realise the damage, moral and material, which could be inflicted on any selected part of the front if it were constantly scoured by a few dozen of such guerrilla raiders. No movement could take place during the daytime, and nobody could remain in the open for longer than a few minutes.

The seemingly far-fetched speculations above are commonplace enough in the judgment of aeronautical people of far greater authority and experience than I can claim. But they could only be brought to materialisation by an abnormal supply of modern aeroplanes, especially the chaser craft necessary to keep German machines from interference. Given the workshop effort to provide this supply, French and British pilots can be relied upon to make the most of it. I am convinced that war flying will be organised as a means to victory; but as my opinion is of small expert value I do not propose to discuss how it might be done. This much, however, I will predict. When, in some nine months' time—if the gods permit—a sequel to the present book appears, dealing with this year's personal experiences above the scene of battle, the aerial factor will be well on the way to the position of war predominance to which it is destined.

Contact.

France, 1917.

Introduction

BY MAJOR-GENERAL W. S. BRANCKER

(Deputy Director-General of Military Aeronautics)

Every day adds something to the achievements of aviation, brings to light yet another of its possibilities, or discloses more vividly its inexhaustible funds of adventure and romance.

This volume, one of the first books about fighting in the air, is written by a fighting airman. The author depicts the daily life of the flying officer in France, simply and with perfect truth; indeed he describes heroic deeds with such moderation and absence of exaggeration that the reader will scarcely realise that these stories are part of the annals of a squadron which for a time held a record in the heaviness of its losses.

The importance of the aerial factor in the prosecution of the war grows apace. The Royal Flying Corps, from being an undependable and weakly assistant to the other arms, is now absolutely indispensable, and has attained a position of almost predominant importance. If the war goes on without decisive success being obtained by our armies on the earth, it seems almost inevitable that we must depend on offensive action in the air and from the air to bring us victory.

We in London have had some slight personal experience of what a very weak and moderately prosecuted aerial offensive can accomplish. With the progress of the past three years before us, it needs little imagination to visualise the possibilities of such an offensive, even in one year's time; and as each succeeding year adds to the power of rival aerial fleets, the thought of war will become almost impossible.

War has been the making of aviation; let us hope that aviation will be the destruction of war.

W. S. Brancker.

August 1, 1917.

CHAPTER 1

Flying to France

All units of the army have known it, the serio-comedy of waiting for embarkation orders.

After months of training the twelvetieth battalion, battery, or squadron is almost ready for a plunge into active service. Then comes, from a source which cannot be trailed, a mysterious Date. The orderly-room whispers: "June the fifteenth"; the senior officers' quarters murmur: "France on June the fifteenth"; the mess echoes to the tidings spread by the subaltern-who-knows: "We're for it on June the fifteenth, me lad"; through the men's hutments the word is spread: "It's goodbye to this blinking hole on June the fifteenth"; the Home receives a letter and confides to other homes: "Reginald's lot are going to the war on June the fifteenth"; finally, if we are to believe Mr. William le Queux, the Military Intelligence Department of the German Empire dockets a report:

Das zwölfzigste Battalion (Batterie oder Escadrille) geht am 15 Juni nach Frankreich.

June opens with an overhaul of officers and men. Last leave is distributed, the doctor examines everybody by batches, backward warriors are worried until they become expert, the sergeant-major polishes his men on the grindstone of discipline, the C.O. indents for a draft to complete establishment, an inspection is held by an awesome general. Except for the mobilisation stores everything is complete by June 10.

But there is still no sign of the wanted stores on the date, and June 16 finds the unit still in the same blinking hole, wherever that may be. The days drag on, and date the second is placed on a pedestal.

"Many thanks for an extra fortnight in England," says the subaltern-who-knows; "we're not going till June the twenty-seventh."

The adjutant, light duty, is replaced by an adjutant, general service. Mobilisation stores begin to trickle into the quartermaster's reservoir. But on June 27 the stores are far from ready, and July 6 is miraged as the next date. This time it looks like business. The war equipment is completed, except for the identity discs.

On July 4 a large detachment departs, after twelve hours' notice, to replace casualties in France. Those remaining in the now incomplete unit grow wearily sarcastic. More last leave is granted. The camp is given over to rumour. An orderly, delivering a message to the C.O. (formerly stationed in India) at the latter's quarters, notes a light cotton tunic and two sun-helmets. Sun-helmets? Ah, somewhere East, of course. The men tell each other forthwith that their destination has been changed to Mesopotamia.

A band of strangers report in place of the draft that went to France, and in them the N.C.O.'s plant *esprit de corps* and the fear of God. The missing identity discs arrive, and a fourth Date is fixed—July 21. And the dwellers in the blinking hole, having been wolfed several times, are sceptical, and treat the latest report as a bad joke.

"My dear man," remarks the subaltern-who-knows, "it's only some more hot air. I never believed in the other dates, and I don't believe in this. If there's one day of the three hundred and sixty-five when we shan't go, it's July the twenty-first."

And at dawn on July 21 the battalion, battery, or squadron moves unobtrusively to a port of embarkation for France.

Whereas in most branches of the army the foundation of this scaffolding of postponement is indistinct except to the second-sighted Staff, in the case of the Flying Corps it is definitely based on that uncertain quantity, the supply of aeroplanes. The organisation of personnel is not a difficult task, for all are highly trained beforehand. The pilots have passed their tests and been decorated with wings, and the mechanics have already learned their separate trades as riggers, fitters, carpenters, sailmakers, and the like. The only training necessary for the pilot is to fly as often as possible on the type of bus he will use in France, and to benefit by the experience of the flight-commanders, who as a rule have spent a hundred or two hours over Archie and the enemy lines. As regards the mechanics, the quality of their skilled work is tempered by the technical sergeant-major, who knows most things about an aeroplane, and the quality of their behaviour by the disciplinary sergeant-major, usually an ex-regular with a lively talent for blasting.

The machines comprise a less straight-forward problem. The new service squadron is probably formed to fly a recently adopted type of aeroplane, of which the early production in quantities is hounded by difficulty. The engine and its parts, the various sections of the machine itself, the guns, the synchronising gear, all these are made in separate factories, after standardisation, and must then be co-ordinated before the craft is ready for its test. If the output of any one part fall below what was expected, the whole is kept waiting; and invariably the quantity or quality of output is at first below expectation in some particular. Adding to the delays of supply others due to the more urgent claims of squadrons at the front for machines to replace those lost or damaged, it can easily be seen that a new squadron will have a succession of dates.

Even when the machines are ready, and the transport leaves with stores, ground-officers, and mechanics, the period of postponement is not ended. All being well, the pilots will fly their craft to France on the day after their kit departs with the transport. But the day after produces impossible weather, as do the five or six days that follow. One takes advantage of each of these set-backs to pay a further farewell visit to one's dearest or nearest, according to where the squadron is stationed, until at the last the dearest or nearest says: "Goodbye. I do hope you'll have a safe trip to France tomorrow morning. You'll come and see me again tomorrow evening, won't you?"

At last a fine morning breaks the spell of dud weather, and the pilots fly away; but lucky indeed is the squadron that reaches France without delivering over part of its possessions to that aerial highwayman the forced landing.

It was at an aerodrome forty minutes distant from London that we patiently waited for flying orders. Less than the average delay was expected, for two flights of the squadron were already on the Somme, and we of the third flight were to join them immediately we received our full complement of war machines. These, in those days, were to be the latest word in fighting two-seaters of the period. Two practice buses had been allotted to us, and on them the pilots were set to perform landings, split-"air" turns, and stunts likely to be useful in a scrap. For the rest, we sorted ourselves out, which pilot was to fly with which observer, and improved the machines' accessories.

An inspiration suggested to the flight-commander, who although an ex-Civil Servant was a man of resource, that mirrors of polished steel, as used on the handlebars of motor-cycles, to give warning of road-craft at the rear, might be valuable in an aeroplane. Forthwith he screwed one to the sloping half-strut of his top centre-section. The trial was a great success, and we bought six such mirrors, an investment which was to pay big dividends in many an air flight.

Next the flight-commander made up his mind to bridge the chasm of difficult communication between pilot and observer. Formerly, in two-seaters with the pilot's seat in front, a message could only be delivered on a slip of paper or by shutting off the engine, so that one's voice could be heard; the loss of time in each case being ill afforded when Huns were near. An experiment with a wide speaking-tube, similar to those through which a waiter in a Soho restaurant demands *côtelettes milanèses* from an underground kitchen, had proved that the engine's roar was too loud for distinct transmission by this means. We made a mouthpiece and a sound-box earpiece, and tried them on tubes of every make and thickness; but whenever the engine was at work the words sounded indistinct as words sung in English Opera.

One day a speedometer behaved badly, and a mechanic was connecting a new length of the rubber pitot-tubing along which the air is sucked from a wingtip to operate the instrument. Struck with an idea, the pilot fitted mouthpiece and earpiece to a stray piece of the tubing, and took to the air with his observer. The pair conversed easily and pleasantly all the way to 10,000 feet. The problem was solved, and ever afterwards pilot and observer were able to warn and curse each other in mid-air without waste of time. The high-powered two-seaters of today are supplied with excellent speaking-tubes before they leave the factories; but we, who were the first to use a successful device of this kind on active service, owed its introduction to a chance idea.

One by one our six war machines arrived and were allotted to their respective pilots. Each man treated his bus as if it were an only child. If another pilot were detailed to fly it the owner would watch the performance jealously, and lurid indeed was the subsequent talk if an outsider choked the carburettor, taxied the bus on the switch, or otherwise did something likely to reduce the efficiency of engine or aeroplane. On the whole, however, the period of waiting was dull, so that we welcomed comic relief provided by the affair of the Jabberwocks.

The first three machines delivered from the Rafborough *depôt* disappointed us in one particular. The movable mounting for the observer's gun in the rear cockpit was a weird contraption like a giant catapult. It occupied a great deal of room, was stiff-moving, reduced the speed by about five miles an hour owing to head resistance, refused to be slewed round sideways for sighting at an angle, and constantly collided with the observer's head. We called it the Christmas Tree, the Heath Robinson, the Jabberwock, the Ruddy Limit, and names unprintable. The next three buses were fitted with Scarff mountings, which were as satisfactory as the Jabberwocks were unsatisfactory.

Then, late in the evening, one of the new craft was crashed beyond repair. At early dawn a pilot and his observer left their beds, walked through the rain to the aerodrome, and sneaked to the flight shed. They returned two hours later, hungry, dirty, and flushed with suppressed joy. After breakfast we found that the crashed bus had lost a Scarff mounting, and the bus manned by the early risers had found one. The gargoyle shape of a discarded Jabberwock sprawled on the floor.

At lunch-time another pilot disappeared with his observer and an air of determination. When the shed was opened for the afternoon's work the Jabberwock had been replaced on the machine of the early risers, and the commandeered Scarff was affixed neatly to the machine of the quick-lunchers. While the two couples slanged each other a third pilot and observer sought out the flight-commander, and explained why they were entitled to the disputed mounting. The pilot, the observer pointed out, was the senior pilot of the three; the observer, the pilot pointed out, was the senior observer. Was it not right, therefore, that they should be given preferential treatment? The flight-commander agreed, and by the time the early-risers and quick-lunchers had settled their quarrel by the spin of a coin, the Scarff had found a fourth and permanent home.

The two remaining Jabberwocks became an obsession with their unwilling owners, who hinted darkly at mutiny when told that no more Scarffs could be obtained, the Naval Air Service having contracted for all the new ones in existence. But chance, in the form of a Big Bug's visit of inspection, opened the way for a last effort. In the machine examined by the Big Bug, an exhausted observer was making frantic efforts to swivel an archaic framework from back to front. The Big Bug looked puzzled, but passed on without comment. As he approached the next machine a second observer tried desperately to move a similar monstrosity round its hinges, while the pilot, stop-watch in hand, looked on with evident sorrow. The Big Bug now decided to investigate, and he demanded the reason for the stop-watch and the hard labour.

"We've just timed this mounting, sir, to see how quickly it could be moved for firing at a Hun. I find it travels at the rate of 6.5 inches a minute."

"Disgraceful," said the Big Bug. "We'll get them replaced by the new type." And get them replaced he did, the R.N.A.S. contract notwithstanding. The four conspirators have since believed themselves to be heaven-born strategists.

Followed the average number of delays due to crashed aeroplanes and late stores. At length, however, the transport moved away with our equipment, and we received orders to proceed by air a day later. But next day brought a steady drizzle, which continued for some forty-eight hours, so that instead of proceeding by air the kitless officers bought clean collars. Then came two days of low, clinging mist, and the purchase of shirts. A fine morning on the fifth day forestalled the necessity of new pyjamas.

At ten of the clock we were in our machines, saying good-bye to a band of lucky pilots who stayed at home to strafe the Zeppelin and be petted in the picture press and the Piccadilly grillroom. "Contaxer!" called a mechanic, facing the flight-commander's propeller. "Contact!" replied the flight-commander; his engine roared, around flew the propeller, the chocks were pulled clear, and away and up raced the machine. The rest followed and took up their appointed places behind the leader, at a height chosen for the rendezvous.

We headed in a south-easterly direction, passing on our left the ragged fringe of London. At this point the formation was not so good as it might have been, probably because we were taking leave of the Thames and other landmarks. But four of the twelve who comprised the party have since seen them, and of these four one was to return by way of a German hospital, a prison camp, a jump from the footboard of a train, a series of lone night-walks that extended over two months, and an escape across the frontier of *Neutralia*, while two fellow-fugitives were shot dead by Boche sentries.

Above the junction of Redhill the leader veered to the left and steered by railway to the coast. Each pilot paid close attention to his place in the group, for this was to be a test of whether our formation flying was up to the standard necessary for work over enemy country. To keep exact formation is far from easy for the novice who has to deal with the vagaries of a rotary engine in a machine sensitive on the controls. The engine develops a sudden increase of revolutions, and the pilot finds himself overhauling the craft in front; he throttles back and finds himself being overhauled by the craft behind; a slight deviation from the course and the craft all around seem to be swinging sideways or upwards. Not till a pilot can fly his bus unconsciously does he keep place without repeated reference to the throttle and instrument-board.

Beyond Redhill we met an unwieldy cloudbank and were forced to lose height. The clouds became denser and lower, and the formation continued to descend, so that when the coast came into view we were below 3000 feet.

A more serious complication happened near Dovstone, the port which was to be our cross-Channel springboard. There we ran into a mist, thick as a London fog. It covered the Channel like a blanket, and completely enveloped Dovstone and district. To cross under these conditions would have been absurd, for opaque vapour isolated us from the ground and cut the chain of vision which had bound together the six machines. We dropped through the pall of mist and trusted to Providence to save us from collision.

Four fortunate buses emerged directly above Dovstone aerodrome, where they landed. The other two, in one of which I was a passenger, came out a hundred feet over the cliffs. We turned inland, and soon found ourselves travelling over a wilderness of roofs and chimneys. A church-tower loomed ahead, so we climbed back into the mist. Next we all but crashed into the hill south of Dovstone. We banked steeply and swerved to the right, just as the slope seemed rushing towards us through the haze.

Once more we descended into the clear air. Down below was a large field, and in the middle of it was an aeroplane. Supposing this to be the aerodrome, we landed, only to find ourselves in an uneven meadow, containing, besides the aeroplane already mentioned, one cow, one pond, and some Brass Hats.[1] As the second bus was taxiing over the grass the pilot jerked it round sharply to avoid the pond. His undercarriage gave, the propeller hit the earth and smashed itself, and the machine heeled over and pulled up dead, with one wing leaning on the ground.

Marmaduke, our war baby, was the pilot of the maimed machine. He is distinctly young, but he can on occasion declaim impassioned language in a manner that would be creditable to the most liver-ridden major in the Indian Army. The Brass Hats seemed mildly surprised when, after inspecting the damage, Marmaduke danced around

1. Officers from Headquarters.

the unfortunate bus and cursed systematically persons and things so diverse as the thingumy fool whose machine had misled us into landing, the thingumy pond, the thingumy weather expert who ought to have warned us of the thingumy Channel mist, the *Kaiser*, his aunt, and his contemptible self.

He was no what-you-may-call-it good as a pilot, shouted Marmaduke to the ruminative cow, and he intended to leave the blank R.F.C. for the Blanky Army Service Corps or the blankety Gravediggers Corps. As a last resort, he would get a job as a double-blank Cabinet Minister, being no blank-blank good for anything else.

The Brass Hats gazed and gazed and gazed. A heavy silence followed Marmaduke's outburst, a silence pregnant with possibilities of Staff displeasure, of summary arrest, of—laughter. Laughter won. The Brass Hats belonged to the staff of an Anzadian division in the neighbourhood, and one of them, a young-looking major with pink riding breeches and a prairie accent, said—

"Gentlemen, some beautiful birds, some beautiful swear, and, by Abraham's trousers, some beautiful angel boy."

Marmaduke wiped the foam from his mouth and apologised.

"Not at all," said the Brass Hat from one of our great Dominions of Empire, "I do it every day myself, before breakfast generally."

Meanwhile the news of our arrival had rippled the calm surface of the daily round at Dovstone. Obviously, said the good people to each other, the presence of three aeroplanes in a lonely field, with a guard of Anzadians around the said field, must have some hidden meaning. Perhaps there had been a German air raid under cover of the mist. Perhaps a German machine had been brought down. Within half an hour of our erratic landing a dozen people in Dovstone swore to having seen a German aeroplane touch earth in our field. The pilot had been made prisoner by Anzadians, added the dozen eye-witnesses.

Such an event clearly called for investigation by Dovstone's detective intellects. We were honoured by a visit from two special constables, looking rather like the Bing Boys. Their collective eagle eye grasped the situation in less than a second. I happened to be standing in the centre of the group, still clad in flying kit. The Bing Boys decided that I was their prey, and one of them advanced, flourishing a note-book.

"Excuse me, sir," said he to a Brass Hat, "I represent the civil authority. Will you please tell me if this"—pointing to me—"is the captive baby-killer?"

"Now give us the chorus, old son," said Marmaduke. Explanations followed, and the Bing Boys retired, rather crestfallen.

It is embarrassing enough to be mistaken for a German airman. It is more embarrassing to be mistaken for an airman who shot down a German airman when there was no German airman to shoot down. Such was the fate of the four of us—two pilots and two observers—when we left our field to the cow and the conference of Brass Hats, and drove to the Grand Hotel. The taxi-driver, who, from his enthusiastic civility, had clearly never driven a cab in London, would not be convinced.

"No, sir," he said, when we arrived at the hotel, "I'm proud to have driven you, and I don't want your money. No, sir, I know you *avi-yaters* are modest and aren't allowed to say what you've done. Good day, gentlemen, and good luck, gentlemen."

It was the same in the Grand Hotel. Porters and waiters asked what had become of "the Hun," and no denial could fully convince them. At a *tango* tea held in the hotel that afternoon we were pointed out as the intrepid birdmen who had done the deed of the day. Flappers and fluff-girls further embarrassed us with interested glances, and one of them asked for autographs.

Marmaduke rose to the occasion. He smiled, produced a gold-tipped fountain-pen, and wrote with a flourish, "John James Christopher Benjamin Brown. Greetings from Dovstone."

But Marmaduke the volatile was doomed to suffer a loss of dignity. He had neglected to bring an emergency cap, which an airman on a cross-country flight should never forget. Bareheaded he accompanied us to a hatter's. Here the R.F.C. caps of the "stream-lined" variety had all been sold, so the war baby was obliged to buy a general service hat. The only one that fitted him was shapeless as a *hausfrau*, ponderous as a Bishop, unstable as a politician, grotesque as a Birthday Honours' List. It was a nice quiet hat, we assured Marmaduke—just the thing for active service. Did it suit him? Very well indeed, we replied—made him look like Lord Haldane at the age of sixteen. Marmaduke bought it.

The monstrosity brought us a deal of attention in the streets, but this Marmaduke put down to his fame as a conqueror of phantom raiders. He began, however, to suspect that something was wrong when a newsboy shouted, "Where jer get that 'at, leftenant?" The question was unoriginal and obvious; but the newsboy showed imagination at his second effort, which was the opening line of an old music-hall chorus: "Sidney's 'olidays er in Septembah!" Marmaduke called at another shop and chose the stiffest hat he could find.

By next morning the mist had cleared, and we flew across the Channel, under a curtain of clouds, leaving Marmaduke to fetch a new machine. When you visit the Continent after the war, friend the reader, travel by the Franco-British service of aerial transport, which will come into being with the return of peace. You will find it more comfortable and less tiring; and if you have a weak stomach you will find it less exacting, for none but the very nervous are ill in an aeroplane, if the pilot behaves himself. Also, you will complete the journey in a quarter of the time taken by boat. Within fifteen minutes of our departure from Dovstone we were in French air country. A few ships specked the sea-surface, which reflected a dull grey from the clouds, but otherwise the crossing was monotonous.

We passed up the coast-line as far as the bend at Cape Grisnez, and so to Calais. Beyond this town were two sets of canals, one leading south and the other east. Follow the southern group and you will find our immediate destination, the aircraft depôt at Saint Gregoire. Follow the eastern group and they will take you to the Boche aircraft depôt at Lille. Thus were we reminded that tango teas and special constables belonged to the past.

The covey landed at Saint Gregoire without mishap, except for a bent axle and a torn tyre. With these replaced, and the supplies of petrol and oil replenished, we flew south during the afternoon to the river-basin of war. Marmaduke arrived five days later, in time to take part in our first patrol over the lines. On this trip his engine was put out of action by a stray fragment from anti-aircraft. After gliding across the trenches, he landed among some dug-outs inhabited by sappers, and made use of much the same vocabulary as when he crashed at Dovstone Marmaduke shot down several Hun machines during the weeks that followed, but on the very day of his posting for a decoration a Blighty bullet gave him a return ticket to England and a mention in the casualty list. When last I heard of him he was at Dovstone aerodrome, teaching his elders how to fly. I can guess what he would do if at the Grand Hotel there some chance-introduced collector of autographs offered her book. He would think of the cow and the Brass Hats, smile, produce his gold-tipped fountain-pen, and write with a flourish, "John James Christopher Benjamin Brown. Greetings from Dovstone."

CHAPTER 2

The Day's Work

For weeks we had talked guardedly of "it" and "them"—of the greatest day of the Push and the latest form of warfare. Details of the twin mysteries had been rightly kept secret by the red-hatted Olympians who really knew, though we of the fighting branches had heard sufficient to stimulate an appetite for rumour and exaggeration. Consequently we possessed our souls in impatience and dabbled in conjecture.

Small forts moving on the caterpillar system of traction used for heavy guns were to crawl across No Man's Land, enfilade the enemy front line with quick-firing and machine guns, and hurl bombs on such of the works and emplacements as they did not ram to pieces,— thus a confidential adjutant, who seemed to think he had admitted me into the inner circle of knowledge tenanted only by himself and the G.S.O. people (1., 2., and 3., besides untabbed nondescripts). Veterans gave tips on war in the open country, or chatted airily about another tour of such places as Le Catelet, Le Cateau, Mons, the Maubeuge district, and Namur. The cautious listened in silence, and distilled only two facts from the dubious mixture of fancy. The first was that we were booked for a big advance one of these fine days; and the second that new armoured cars, caterpillared and powerfully armed, would make their bow to Brother Boche.

The balloon of swollen conjecture floated over the back of the Front until it was destroyed by the quick-fire of authentic orders, which necessarily revealed much of the plan and many of the methods. On the afternoon of September 14 all the officers of our aerodrome were summoned to an empty shed. There we found our own particular General, who said more to the point in five minutes than the rumourists had said in five weeks. There was to be a grand attack next morning. The immediate objectives were not distant, but their gain would be of enormous value. Every atom of energy must be concentrated on the task. It was hoped that an element of surprise would be on our side, helped by a new engine of war christened the Tank. The nature of this strange animal, male and female, was then explained.

Next came an exposition of the part allotted to the Flying Corps. No German machines could be allowed near enough to the lines for any observation. We must shoot all Hun machines at sight and give them no rest. Our bombers should make life a burden on the enemy lines of communication. Infantry and transport were to be worried, whenever possible, by machine-gun fire from above. Machines would be detailed for contact work with our infantry. Reconnaissance jobs were to be completed at all costs, if there seemed the slightest chance of bringing back useful information.

No more bubbles of hot air were blown around the mess table. Only the evening was between us and the day of days. The time before dinner was filled by the testing of machines and the writing of those cheerful, non-committal letters that precede big happenings at the front. Our flight had visitors to dinner, but the shadow of tomorrow was too insistent for the racket customary on a guest night. It was as if the electricity had been withdrawn from the atmosphere and condensed for use when required. The dinner talk was curiously restrained. The usual shop chatter prevailed, leavened by snatches of bantering cynicism from those infants of the world who thought that to be a *beau sabreur* of the air one must juggle verbally with life, death, and Archie shells.

Even these war babies (three of them died very gallantly before we reassembled for breakfast next day) had bottled most of their exuberance. Understanding silences were sandwiched between yarns. A wag searched for the Pagliacci record, and set the gramophone to churn out "*Vesti la Giubba.*" The guests stayed to listen politely to a few revue melodies, and then slipped away. The rest turned in immediately, in view of the jobs at early dawn.

"Night, everybody," said one of the flight-commanders. "Meet you at Mossy-Face in the morning!"

In the morning some of us saw him spin earthwards over Mossy-Face Wood, surrounded by Hun machines.

Long before the dawn of September 15, I awoke to the roar of engines, followed by an overhead drone as a party of bombers circled round until they were ready to start. When this noise had died away, the dull boom of an intense bombardment was able to make itself heard. I rolled over and went to sleep again, for our own show was not due to start until three hours later.

The Flying Corps programme on the great day was a marvel of organisation. The jobs fitted into one another, and into the general tactical scheme of the advance, as exactly as the parts of a flawless motor. At no time could enemy craft steal toward the lines to spy out the land. Every sector was covered by defensive patrols which travelled northward and southward, southward and northward, eager to pounce on any black-crossed stranger. Offensive patrols moved and fought over Boche territory until they were relieved by other offensive patrols. The machines on artillery observation were thus worried only by Archie, and the reconnaissance formations were able to do their work with little interruption, except when they passed well outside the patrol areas.

Throughout the day those guerrillas of the air, the bombing craft, went across and dropped eggs on anything between general headquarters and a railway line. The corps buses kept constant communication between attacking battalions and the rear. A machine first reported the exploit of the immortal Tank that waddled down High Street, Flers, spitting bullets and inspiring sick fear. And there were many free-lance stunts, such as Lewis gun attacks on reserve troops or on trains.

The three squadrons attached to our aerodrome had to the day's credit two long reconnaissances, three offensive patrols, and four bomb raids. Six Hun machines were destroyed on these shows, and the bombers did magnificent work at vital points. At 2 a.m. they dropped eggs on the German Somme headquarters. An hour later they deranged the railway station of a large garrison town. For the remaining time before sunset they were not so busy. They merely destroyed an ammunition train, cut two railway lines, damaged an important railhead, and sprayed a bivouac ground.

An orderly called me at 4.15 a.m. for the big offensive patrol. The sky was a dark-grey curtain decorated by faintly twinkling stars. I dressed to the thunderous accompaniment of the guns, warmed myself with a cup of hot cocoa, donned flying kit, and hurried to the aerodrome. There we gathered around C., the patrol leader, who gave us final instructions about the method of attack. We tested our guns and climbed into the machines.

By now the east had turned to a light grey with pink smudges from the forefinger of sunrise. Punctually at five o'clock the order, "Start up!" passed down the long line of machines. The flight-commander's engine began a loud metallic roar, then softened as it was throttled down. The pilot waved his hand, the chocks were pulled from under the wheels, and the machine moved forward. The throttle was again opened full out as the bus raced into the wind until flying speed had been attained, when it skimmed gently from the ground. We followed, and carried out the rendezvous at 3000 feet.

The morning light increased every minute, and the grey of the sky was merging into blue. The faint, hovering ground-mist was not sufficient to screen our landmarks. The country below was a shadowy patchwork of coloured pieces. The woods, fantastic shapes of dark green, stood out strongly from the mosaic of brown and green fields. The pattern was divided and subdivided by the straight, poplar-bordered roads peculiar to France.

We passed on to the dirty strip of wilderness which is the actual front. The battered villages and disorderly ruins looked like hieroglyphics traced on wet sand. A sea of smoke rolled over the ground for miles. It was a by-product of one of the most terrific bombardments in the history of trench warfare. Through it hundreds of gun-flashes twinkled, like the lights of a Chinese garden.

Having reached a height of 12,000 feet, we crossed the trenches south of Bapaume. As the danger that stray bullets might fall on friends no longer existed, pilots and observers fired a few rounds into space to make sure their guns were behaving properly.

Archie began his frightfulness early. He concentrated on the leader's machine, but the still-dim light spoiled his aim, and many of the bursts were dotted between the craft behind. I heard the customary *wouff! wouff! wouff!* followed in one case by the *hs-s-s-s-s* of passing fragments. We swerved and dodged to disconcert the gunners. After five minutes of hide-and-seek, we shook off this group of Archie batteries.

The flight-commander headed for Mossy-Face Wood, scene of many air battles and bomb raids. An aerodrome just east of the wood was the home of the Fokker star, Boelcke. C. led us to it, for it was his great ambition to account for Germany's best pilot.

While we approached, I looked down and saw eight machines with black Maltese crosses on their planes, about three thousand feet below. They had clipped wings of a peculiar whiteness, and they were ranged one above the other, like the rungs of a Venetian blind. A cluster of small scouts swooped down from Heaven-knows-what height and hovered above us; but C. evidently did not see them, for he dived steeply on the Huns underneath, accompanied by the two machines nearest him. The other group of enemies then dived.

I looked up and saw a narrow biplane, apparently a Roland, rushing towards our bus. My pilot turned vertically and then side-slipped to disconcert the Boche's aim. The black-crossed craft swept over at a distance of less than a hundred yards. I raised my gun-mounting, sighted, and pressed the trigger. Three shots rattled off—and my Lewis gun ceased fire.

Intensely annoyed at being cheated out of such a splendid target, I applied immediate action, pulled back the cocking-handle and pressed the trigger again. Nothing happened. After one more immediate action test, I examined the gun and found that an incoming cartridge and an empty case were jammed together in the breech. To remedy the stoppage, I had to remove spade-grip and body cover. As I did this, I heard an ominous *ta-ta-ta-ta-ta* from the returning German scout. My pilot cart-wheeled round and made for the Hun, his gun spitting continuously through the propeller. The two machines raced at each other until less than fifty yards separated them. Then the Boche swayed, turned aside, and put his nose down. We dropped after him, with our front machine-gun still speaking. The Roland's glide merged into a dive, and we imitated him. Suddenly a streak of flame came from his petrol tank, and the next second he was rushing earthwards, with two streamers of smoke trailing behind.

I was unable to see the end of this vertical dive, for two more single-seaters were upon us. They plugged away while I remedied the stoppage, and several bullets ventilated the fuselage quite close to my cockpit. When my gun was itself again, I changed the drum of ammunition, and hastened to fire at the nearest Hun. He was evidently unprepared, for he turned and moved across our tail. As he did so, I raked his bus from stem to stern. I looked at him hopefully, for the range was very short, and I expected to see him drop towards the ground at several miles a minute. He sailed on serenely. This is an annoying habit of enemy machines when one is sure that, by the rules of the game, they ought to be destroyed.

The machine in question was probably hit, however, for it did not return, and I saw it begin a glide as though the pilot meant to land. We switched our attention to the remaining Hun, but this one was not anxious to fight alone. He dived a few hundred feet, with tail well up, looking for all the world like a trout when it drops back into water.

Afterwards he flattened out and went east.

During the fight we had become separated from the remainder of our party. I searched all round the compass, but could find neither friend nor foe. We returned to the aerodrome where hostile craft were first sighted. There was no sign of C.'s machine or of the others who dived on the first group of Huns. Several German machines were at rest in the aerodrome.

Finding ourselves alone, we passed on towards the lines. I twisted my neck in every direction, for over enemy country only a constant look out above, below, and on all sides can save a machine from a surprise attack. After a few minutes, we spotted six craft bearing towards us from a great height. Through field-glasses I was able to see their black crosses, and I fingered my machine-gun expectantly.

The strangers dived in two lots of three. I waited until the first three were within 300 yards' range and opened fire. One of them swerved away, but the other two passed right under us. Something sang to the right, and I found that part of a landing-wire was dangling helplessly from its socket. We thanked whatever gods there be that it was not a flying-wire, and turned to meet the next three Huns. We swerved violently, and they pulled out of their dive well away from us. With nose down and engine full out, we raced towards the lines and safety. Three of the attackers were unable to keep up with us and we left them behind.

The other three Germans, classed by my pilot as Halberstadts, had a great deal more speed than ours. They did not attack at close quarters immediately, but flew 200 to 300 yards behind, ready to pounce at their own moment. Two of them got between my gun and our tail-plane, so that they were safe from my fire. The third was slightly above our height, and for his benefit I stood up and rattled through a whole ammunition-drum. Here let me say I do not think I hit him, for he was not in difficulties. He dived below us to join his companions, possibly because he did not like being under fire when they were not. To my surprise and joy, he fell slick on one of the other two Hun machines. This latter broke into two pieces, which fell like stones. The machine responsible for my luck side-slipped, spun a little, recovered, and went down to land. The third made off east.

In plain print and at a normal time, this episode shows little that is comic. But when it happened I was in a state of high tension, and this, combined with the startling realisation that a Hun pilot had saved me and destroyed his friend, seemed irresistibly comic. I cackled with laughter and was annoyed because my pilot did not see the joke.

We reached the lines without further trouble from anything but Archie. The pink streaks of daybreak had now disappeared beneath the whole body of the sunrise, and the sky was of that intense blue which is the secret of France. What was left of the ground-mist shimmered as it congealed in the sunlight. The pall of smoke from the guns had doubled in volume. The Ancre sparkled brightly.

We cruised around in a search for others of our party, but found none. A defensive patrol was operating between Albert and the trenches. We joined it for half an hour, at the end of which I heard a "Halloa!" from the speaking-tube.

"What's up now?" I asked.

"Going to have a look at the war," was the pilot's reply.

Before I grasped his meaning he had shut off the engine and we were gliding towards the trenches. At 1200 feet we switched on, flattened out, and looked for movement below. There was no infantry advance at the moment, but below Courcelette what seemed to be two ungainly masses of black slime were slithering over the ground. I rubbed my eyes and looked again. One of them actually crawled among the scrap-heaps that fringed the ruins of the village. Only then did the thought that they might be Tanks suggest itself. Afterwards I discovered that this was so.

The machine rocked violently as a projectile hurtled by underneath us. The pilot remembered the broken landing-wire and steered for home. After landing, we compared notes with others who had returned from the expedition. C., we learned, was down at last, after seventeen months of flying on active service, with only one break for any appreciable time. He destroyed one more enemy before the Boches got him. In the dive he got right ahead of the two machines that followed him. As these hurried to his assistance, they saw an enemy plane turn over, show a white, gleaming belly, and drop in zigzags. C.'s bus was then seen to heel over into a vertical dive and to plunge down, spinning rhythmically on its axis. Probably he was shot dead and fell over on to the joystick, which put the machine to its last dive. The petrol tank of the second machine to arrive among the Huns was plugged by a bullet, and the pilot was forced to land. Weeks later, his observer wrote us a letter from a prison camp in Hanover. The third bus, perforated by scores of bullet-holes, got back to tell the tale.

C. was one of the greatest pilots produced by the war. He was utterly fearless, and had more time over the German lines to his credit than anyone else in the Flying Corps. It was part of his fatalistic creed that Archie should never be dodged, and he would go calmly ahead when the A.-A. guns were at their best. Somehow, the bursts never found him. He had won both the D.S.O. and the M.C. for deeds in the air. Only the evening before, when asked lightly if he was out for a V.C., he said he would rather get Boelcke than the V.C.; and in the end Boelcke probably got him, for he fell over the famous German pilot's aerodrome, and that day the German wireless announced that Boelcke had shot down two more machines. Peace to the ashes of a fine pilot and a very brave man!

Two observers, other than C.'s passenger, had been killed during our patrol. One of them was "Uncle," a captain in the Northumberland Fusiliers. A bullet entered the large artery of his thigh. He bled profusely and lost consciousness in the middle of a fight with two Huns. When he came to, a few minutes later, he grabbed his gun and opened fire on an enemy. After about forty shots the chatter of the gun ceased, and through the speaking-tube a faint voice told the pilot to look round. The pilot did so, and saw a Maltese-cross biplane falling in flames. But Uncle had faded into unconsciousness again, and he never came back. It is more than possible that if he had put a tourniquet round his thigh, instead of continuing the fight, he might have lived.

A great death, you say? One of many such. Only the day before I had helped to lift the limp body of Paddy from the floor of an observer's cockpit. He had been shot over the heart. He fainted, recovered his senses for ten minutes, and kept two Huns at bay until he died, by which time the trenches were reached.

Imagine yourself under fire in an aeroplane at 10,000 feet. Imagine that only a second ago you were in the country of shadows. Imagine yourself feeling giddy and deadly sick from loss of blood. Imagine what is left of your consciousness to be stabbed insistently by a throbbing pain. Now imagine how you would force yourself in this condition to grasp a machine-gun in your numbed hand, pull back the cocking-handle, take careful aim at a fast machine, allowing for deflection, and fire until you sink into death. Someday I hope to be allowed to visit Valhalla for half an hour, that I may congratulate Paddy and Uncle.

We refreshed ourselves with cold baths and hot breakfast. In the mess the fights were reconstructed. Sudden silences were frequent— an unspoken tribute to C. and the other casualties. But at lunch-time we were cheered by the news that the first and second objectives had been reached, that Martinpuich, Courcelette, and Flers had fallen, and that the Tanks had behaved well.

After lunch I rested awhile before the long reconnaissance, due to start at three. Six machines were detailed for this job; though a faulty engine kept one of them on the ground. The observers marked the course on their maps, and wrote out lists of railway stations. At 3.30 we set off towards Arras.

Archie hit out as soon as we crossed to his side of the front. He was especially dangerous that afternoon, as if determined to avenge the German defeat of the morning. Each bus in turn was encircled by black bursts, and each bus in lost height, swerved, or changed its course to defeat the gunner's aim. A piece of H.E. hit our tail-plane, and stayed there until I cut it out for a souvenir when we had returned.

The observers were kept busy with note-book and pencil, for the train movement was far greater than the average, and streaks of smoke courted attention on all the railways. Rolling stock was correspondingly small, and the counting of the trucks in the sidings was not difficult. Road and canal transport was plentiful. As evidence of the urgency of all this traffic, I remarked that no effort at concealment was made. On ordinary days, a German train always shut off steam when we approached; and often I saw transport passing along the road one minute, and not passing along the road the next. On September 15 the traffic was too urgent for time to be lost by hide-and-seek.

We passed several of our offensive patrols, each of which escorted us while we were on its beat. It was curious that no activity could be noticed on enemy aerodromes. Until we passed Mossy-Face on the last lap of the homeward journey we saw no Hun aircraft. Even there the machines with black crosses flew very low and did not attempt to offer battle.

Nothing out of the ordinary happened until we were about to cross the trenches north of Péronne. Archie then scored an inner. One of his chunks swept the left aileron from the leader's machine, which banked vertically, almost rolled over, and began to spin. For two thousand feet the irregular drop continued, and the observer gave up hope. Luckily for him, the pilot was not of the same mind, and managed to check the spin by juggling with his rudder-controls. The bus flew home, left wing well down, with the observer leaning far out to the right to restore equilibrium, while the icy rush of air boxed his ears.

We landed, wrote our reports, and took them to headquarters. The day's work had been done, which was all that mattered to any extent, and a very able general told us it was "*dom* good." But many a day passed before we grew accustomed to the absence of Uncle and Paddy.

And so to bed, until we were called for another early morning show.

Chapter 3

A Summer Joy-Ride

It happened late in the afternoon, one August dog-day. No wind leavened the languid air, and hut, hangar, tent, and workshop were oppressive with a heavy heat, so that we wanted to sleep. To taxi across the grass in a chase for flying speed, to soar gently from the hot ground, and, by leaning beyond the windscreen, to let the slip-stream of displaced air play on one's face—all this was refreshing as a cold plunge after a Turkish bath. I congratulated myself that I was no longer a gunner, strenuous over interminable corrections, or tiredly alert in a close observation post.

Our party consisted of four machines, each complete with pilot, observer, and several hundred rounds of ammunition. The job was an offensive patrol—that is to say, we were to hunt trouble around a given area behind the Boche lines. A great deal of the credit for our "mastery of the air"—that glib phrase of the question-asking politician—during the Somme Push of 1916, belongs to those who organised and those who led these fighting expeditions over enemy country. Thanks to them, our aircraft were able to carry out reconnaissance, artillery observation, and photography with a minimum of interruption, while the German planes were so hard pressed to defend their place in the air that they could seldom guide their own guns or collect useful information. To this satisfactory result must be added the irritative effect on enemy morale of the knowledge that whenever the weather was fine our machines hummed overhead, ready to molest and be molested.

Offensive patrols are well worth while, but for the comfort of those directly concerned they are rather too exciting. When friends are below during an air duel a pilot is warmly conscious that should he or his machine be crippled he can break away and land, and there's an end of it. But if a pilot be wounded in a scrap far away from home, before he can land he must fly for many miles, under shell fire and probably pursued by enemies. He must conquer the blighting faintness which accompanies loss of blood, keep clear-headed enough to deal instantaneously with adverse emergency, and make an unwilling brain command unwilling hands and feet to control a delicate apparatus. Worst of all, if his engine be put out of action at a spot beyond gliding distance of the lines, there is nothing for it but to descend and tamely surrender. And always he is within reach of that vindictive exponent of frightfulness, Archibald the Ever-Ready.

As we climbed to 4000 feet the machines above threw glints of sunlight on the screen of blue infinity. We ranged ourselves and departed. Passing the red roofs and heart-shaped citadel of Doulens and a jagged wood suggestive of a lion rampant, we followed the straight road to Arras. Arrived there, the leader turned south, for we were not yet high enough. As we moved along the brown band of shell-pocked desolation we continued to climb. Patches of smoke from the guns hovered over the ground at intervals. A score of lazy-looking kite balloons hung motionless.

By the time we reached Albert our height was 12,000 feet, and we steered eastward over the ground gained in the June-July advance. Beyond the scrap-heap that once was Pozières two enormous mine craters showed up, dented into the razed surface, one on either side of the Albert-Bapaume road. Flying very low a few buses were working on trench reconnaissance. The sunshine rebounded from the top of their wings, and against the discoloured earth they looked like fireflies. A mile or so behind the then front lines were the twin villages of Courcelette and Martinpuich, divided only by the road. Already they were badly battered, though, unlike Pozières, they still deserved the title of village. Le Sars, which sat astride the road, nearer Bapaume, had been set afire by our guns, and was smoking.

In those days, before the methodical advance of the British artillery had begun to worry the stronghold overmuch, Bapaume was a hotbed of all the anti-aircraft devilries. We therefore swerved toward the south. Archie was not to be shaken off so easily, and we began a series of erratic deviations as he ringed with black puffs first one machine, then another. The shooting was not particularly good; for although no clouds intervened between the guns and their mark, a powerful sun dazzled the gunners, who must have found difficulty in judging height and direction. From Archie's point of view, the perfect sky is one screened from the sunlight, at 20,000 to 30,000 feet, by a mantle of thin clouds against which aircraft are outlined boldly, like stags on a snow-covered slope.

A few minutes in a south-easterly direction brought us to the Bois d'Havrincourt, a large ungainly wood, the shape of which was something between the ace of spades and the ace of clubs. This we knew as Mossy-Face. The region around it was notorious in R.F.C. messes as being the chief centre of the Boche Flying Corps on the British Front.

From the south-west corner Archie again scattered burst and bark at our group, but his inaccuracy made dodging hardly necessary. A lull followed, and I twisted my neck all round the compass, for, in the presence of hostile aeroplanes, Archie seldom behaves, except when friendly machines are about. Two thousand feet below three biplanes were approaching the wood from the south. Black crosses showed up plainly on their grey-white wings. We dropped into a dive toward the strangers.

Under normal conditions a steep dive imparts a feeling of being hemmed in from every side. One takes a deep breath instinctively, and the novice to flying will grip the fuselage, as if to avoid being crushed. And, indeed, a passenger in a diving aeroplane is hemmed in, by the terrific air-pressure to which the solid surface is subjected. If he attempt to stand up or lean over the side, he will be swept back, after a short struggle, beneath the shelter of wind-screen and fuselage. But when diving on a Hun, I have never experienced this troubled sensation, probably because it has been swamped under the high tension of readiness for the task. All the faculties must be concentrated on opening the attack, since an air duel is often decided in the first few seconds at close quarters.

What happens during these few seconds may depend on a trifle, such as the position of the gun-mounting, an untried drum of ammunition, a slight swerve, or firing a second too soon or too late. An airman should regard his body as part of the machine when there is a prospect of a fight, and his brain, which commands the machine, must be instinctive with insight into what the enemy will attempt.

As we dived, then, I estimated the angle at which we might cross the Boche trio, watched for a change of direction on their part, slewed round the gun-mounting to the most effective setting for what would probably be my arc of fire, and fingered the movable back-sight. At first the Huns held to their course as though quite unconcerned. Later, they began to lose height. Their downward line of flight became steeper and steeper, and so did ours.

Just as our leading bus arrived within range and began to spit bullets through the propeller, a signal rocket streaked from the first Boche biplane, and the trio dived almost vertically, honking the while on Klaxon horns. We were then at about 6000 feet.

We were expecting to see the Huns flatten out, when—"*Wouff! wouff! wouff! wouff! wouff!*" said Archie. The German birds were not hawks at all; they were merely tame decoys used to entice us to a pre-arranged spot, at a height well favoured by A.-A. gunners. The ugly puffs encircled us, and it seemed unlikely that an aeroplane could get away without being caught in a patch of hurtling high explosive. Yet nobody was hit. The only redeeming feature of the villain Archibald is that his deeds are less terrible than his noise, and even this is too flat to be truly frightful. Although I was uncomfortable as we raced away, the chorused *wouffs!* reminded me of an epidemic of coughing I heard in church one winter's Sunday, while a fatuous sermon was read by a dull-voiced vicar.

Mingled with the many black bursts were a few green ones, probably gas shells, for Archie had begun to experiment with the gas habit. Very suddenly a line of fiery rectangles shot up and curved towards us when they had reached three-quarters of their maximum height. They rose and fell within thirty yards of our tail. These were "onions," the flaming rockets which the Boche keeps for any hostile aircraft that can be lured to a height between 4000 and 6000 feet.

I yelled to V., my pilot, that we should have to dodge. We sideslipped and swerved to the left. A minute later the stream of onions had disappeared, greatly to my relief, for the prospect of a fire in the air inspires in me a mortal funk. Soon we were to pass from the unpleasant possibility to the far more unpleasant reality.

Once outside the unhealthy region, we climbed to a less dangerous height. Again we became the target for a few dozen H.E. shells. We broke away and swooped downward. Some little distance ahead, and not far below, was a group of five Albatross two-seaters. V. pointed our machine at them, in the wake of the flight-commander's bus.

Next instant the fuselage shivered. I looked along the inside of it and found that a burning shell fragment was lodged on a longeron, half-way between my cockpit and the tail-plane. A little flame zigzagged over the fabric, all but died away, but, being fanned by the wind as we lost height, recovered and licked its way toward the tail. I was too far away to reach the flame with my hands, and the fire extinguisher was by the pilot's seat. I called for it into the speaking-tube. The pilot made no move. Once more I shouted. Again no answer. V.'s earpiece had slipped from under his cap. A thrill of acute fear passed through me as I stood up, forced my arm through the rush of wind, and grabbed V.'s shoulder.

"Fuselage burning! Pass the fire extinguisher!" I yelled.

My words were drowned in the engine's roar; and the pilot, intent on getting near the Boches, thought I had asked which one we were to attack.

"Look out for those two Huns on the left," he called over his shoulder.

"Pass the fire extinguisher!"

"Get ready to shoot, blast you!"

"Fire extinguisher, you ruddy fool!"

A backward glance told me that the fire was nearing the tail-plane at the one end and my box of ammunition at the other, and was too serious for treatment by the extinguisher unless I could get it at once. Desperately I tried to force myself through the bracing-struts and cross-wires behind my seat. To my surprise, head and shoulders and one arm got to the other side—a curious circumstance, as afterwards I tried repeatedly to repeat this contortionist trick on the ground, but failed every time. There I stuck, for it was impossible to wriggle farther. However, I could now reach part of the fire, and at it I beat with gloved hands.

Within half a minute most of the fire was crushed to death. But a thin streak of flame, outside the radius of my arm, still flickered towards the tail. I tore off one of my gauntlets and swung it furiously on to the burning strip. The flame lessened, rose again when I raised the glove, but died out altogether after I had hit it twice more. The load of fear left me, and I discovered an intense discomfort, wedged in as I was between the two crossed bracing-struts. Five minutes passed before I was able, with many a heave and gasp, to withdraw back to my seat.

By now we were at close grips with the enemy, and our machine and another converged on a Hun. V. was firing industriously. As we turned, he glared at me, and knowing nothing of the fire, shouted: "Why the hell haven't you fired yet?" I caught sight of a Boche bus below us, aimed at it, and emptied a drum in short bursts. It swept away, but not before two of the German observer's bullets had plugged our petrol tank from underneath. The pressure went, and with it the petrol supply. The needle on the rev.-counter quivered to the left as the revolutions dropped, and the engine missed on first one, then two cylinders. V. turned us round, and, with nose down, headed the machine for the trenches. Just then the engine ceased work altogether, and we began to glide down.

All this happened so quickly that I had scarcely realised our plight. Next I began to calculate our chances of reaching the lines before we would have to land. Our height was 9000 feet, and we were just over nine and a half miles from friendly territory. Reckoning the gliding possibilities of our type of bus as a mile to a thousand feet, the odds seemed unfavourable. On the other hand, a useful wind had arisen from the east, and V., a very skilful pilot, would certainly cover all the distance that could be covered.

I located our exact position and searched the map for the nearest spot in the lines. The village of Bouchavesnes was a fraction south of due west, and I remembered that the French had stormed it two days previously. From the shape of the line before this advance, there was evidently a small salient, with Bouchavesnes in the middle of the curve. I scribbled this observation on a scrap of paper, which I handed to V. with the compass direction. V. checked my statements on the map, nodded over his shoulder, and set a course for Bouchavesnes.

Could we do it? I prayed to the gods and trusted to the pilot. Through my mind there flitted impossible plans to be tried if we landed in Boche territory. After setting fire to the machine we would attempt to hide, and then, at night-time, creep along a communication trench to the enemy front line, jump across it in a gap between the sentries, and chance getting by the barbed wire and across No Man's Land. Or we would steal to the Somme, float down-stream, and somehow or other pass the entanglements placed across the river by the enemy. *Wouff! wouff!* Archie was complicating the odds.

Further broodings were checked by the sudden appearance of a German scout. Taking advantage of our plight, its pilot dived steeply from a point slightly behind us. We could not afford to lose any distance by dodging, so V. did the only thing possible—he kept straight on. I raised my gun, aimed at the wicked-looking nose of the attacking craft, and met it with a barrage of bullets. These must have worried the Boche, for he swerved aside when a hundred and fifty yards distant, and did not flatten out until he was beneath the tail of our machine. Afterwards he climbed away from us, turned, and dived once more. For a second time we escaped, owing either to some lucky shots from my gun or to the lack of judgment by the Hun pilot. The scout pulled up and passed ahead of us. It rose and manoeuvred as if to dive from the front and bar the way.

Meanwhile, four specks, approaching from the west, had grown larger and larger, until they were revealed as of the F.E. type—the British "pusher" two-seater. The Boche saw them, and hesitated as they bore down on him. Finding himself in the position of a lion attacked by hunters when about to pounce on a tethered goat, he decided not to destroy, for in so doing he would have laid himself open to destruction. When I last saw him he was racing north-east.

There was now no obstacle to the long glide. As we went lower, the torn ground showed up plainly. From 2000 feet I could almost count the shell-holes. Two battery positions came into view, and near one of them I saw tracks and could distinguish movements by a few tiny dots. It became evident that, barring accident, we should reach the French zone.

When slightly behind the trenches a confused chatter from below told us that machine-guns were trained on the machine. By way of retaliation, I leaned over and shot at what looked like an emplacement. Then came the Boche front line, ragged and unkempt. I fired along an open trench. Although far from fearless as a rule, I was not in the least afraid during the eventful glide. My state of intense "wind up" while the fuselage was burning had apparently exhausted my stock of nervousness. I seemed detached from all idea of danger, and the desolated German trench area might have been a side-show at a fair.

We swept by No Man's Land at a height of 600 feet, crossed the French first- and second-line trenches, and, after passing a small ridge, prepared to settle on an uneven *plateau* covered by high bracken. To avoid landing down wind and downhill, the pilot banked to the right before he flattened out. The bus pancaked gently to earth, ran over the bracken, and stopped two yards from a group of shell-holes. Not a wire was broken. The propeller had been scored by the bracken, but the landing was responsible for no other damage. Taking into consideration the broken ground, the short space at our disposal, and the fact that we landed cross-wind, V. had exhibited wonderful skill.

We climbed out, relieved but cantankerous. V., still ignorant of the fire, wanted to know why my gun was silent during our first fight; and I wanted to know why he hadn't shut off the engine and listened when I shouted for the fire extinguisher. Some French gunners ran to meet us. The sight that met them must have seemed novel, even to a *poilu* of two and a half years' understanding.

Supposing that the aeroplane had crashed, they came to see if we were dead or injured. What they found was one almost complete aeroplane and two leather-coated figures, who cursed each other heartily as they stood side by side, and performed a certain natural function which is publicly represented in Brussels by a famous little statue.

"*Quels types!*" said the first Frenchman to arrive.

An examination of the bus revealed a fair crop of bullet holes through the wings and elevator. A large gap in one side of the fuselage, over a longeron that was charred to powder in parts, bore witness to the fire. Petrol was dripping from the spot where the tank had been perforated. On taking a tin of chocolate from his pocket, V. found it ripped and gaping. He searched the pocket and discovered a bright bullet at the bottom. We traced the adventures of that bullet; it had grazed a strut, cut right through the petrol union, and expended itself on the chocolate tin.

Soon our attention was attracted to several French machines that were passing through a barrage of Archie bursts. The bombardment of an aeroplane arouses only the sporting instinct of the average soldier. His interest, though keen, is directed towards the quality of the shooting and the distance of the shells for their target; his attitude when watching a pigeon-shoot would be much the same. But an airman has experience of what the aeroplane crews must be going through, and his thought is all for them. He knows that dull, loud cough of an Archie shell, the hiss of a flying fragment, the wicked black puffs that creep towards their mark and follow it, no matter where the pilot may swerve.

Should a friendly machine tumble to earth after that rare occurrence, a direct hit, all the sensations of an uncontrolled nose-dive are suggested to his senses. He hears the shriek of the up-rushing air, feels the helpless terror. It hurts him to know that he is powerless to save a friend from certain death. He cannot even withdraw his eyes from the falling craft. I was glad we had not viewed the disaster while we were in the air, for nothing is more unnerving than to see another machine crumbled up by a direct hit when Archie is firing at yourself.

"Me," said a French gunner by my side, "I prefer the artillery." With which sentiment I have often agreed when dodging Archie, though at every other time I prefer the Flying Corps work to all other kinds of fighting.

V. disappeared to phone the Squadron Commander, and I was left with the crippled bus and the crowd of Frenchmen. The *poilus* questioned me on subjects ranging from the customary length of a British officer's moustache to the possible length of the war. Yes, we had been hit in a fight with Boche aeroplanes. Yes, there had also been a slight fire on board. Yes, I had great fear at the time. Yes, I would accept a cigarette with pleasure. No, it was untrue that England contained four million civilian *embusqués* of military age. No, the report that officers of the British Flying Corps received fifty francs a day was inaccurate, unfortunately. But no, my good-for-nothing opinion was that we should not finish the Boche within a year; and so on.

"How is it," said one man in faded uniform, "that the British always manage to keep themselves correct and shaven?"

"*La barbe!*" interrupted another; "the Tommies don't keep clean on the Somme. Even the lilies of the *état-majeur* can't." And he began to quote:

Si ma fi-fi-fiancée me voyait,
Elle m' dirait en me donnant cinq sous:
'Va t' faire raser!' mais moi, j' répondrais
Que moi j'ai toujours les mêmes deux joues.

V. was away for an hour and a half and when he did return it was to announce that he had been unable to phone because the line was blocked under pressure of important operations. Deciding to report in person, we declined an offer of hospitality from the French officers, but gratefully accepted a guard for the machine, and the loan of a car.

A young lieutenant accompanied us as far as Amiens. There we stopped for supper, and were joined by some civilian friends of our French companion. The *filet de sole au vin blanc* engendered a feeling of deep content. Now that it was over, I felt pleased with the day's excitement and the contrast it afforded. Three hours beforehand it seemed likely that the evening would see us prisoners. Yet here we were, supping in a comfortable hotel with three charming ladies and the widow Clicquot.

Arrived at the aerodrome, we visited the hut inhabited by the Squadron Commander, who wore pyjamas and a smile of welcome. We were just in time, he said, to rescue our names from the list of missing. Our tale impressed him so much that, after making arrangements for the stranded bus to be brought back by a repair party, he remarked: "You can both have a rest tomorrow."

"Welcome home, you rotten night-bird," said my tent companion, and mentioned in a hurt tone that our flight was booked for the 5 a.m. reconnaissance. But my last thought before sinking into sleep was of the blessed words: "You can have a rest tomorrow."

Spying Out the Land

For thirty hours the flight had "stood by" for a long reconnaissance. We were dragged from bed at 4.30 of dawn, only to return gratefully beneath the blankets three-quarters of an hour later, when a slight but steady rain washed away all chance of an immediate job. The drizzle continued until after sundown, and our only occupations throughout the day were to wade from mess to aerodrome, aerodrome to mess, and to overhaul in detail machines, maps, guns, and consciences.

Next morning again we dressed in the half-light, and again went back to bed in the daylight. This time the show had been postponed because of low clouds and a thick ground-mist that hung over the reeking earth. It was a depressing dawn—clammy, moist, and sticky.

But by early afternoon the mist had congealed, and the sheet of clouds was torn to rags by a strong south-west wind. The four craft detailed for the reconnaissance were therefore lined outside their shed, while their crews waited for flying orders. I was to be in the leading bus, for when C.'s death left vacant the command of A Flight, the good work of my pilot had brought him a flight-commandership, a three-pipped tunic, and a sense of responsibility which, to my relief, checked his tendency to over-recklessness. He now came from the squadron office with news of a changed course.

"To get the wind behind us," he explained, "we shall cross well to the south of Péronne. Next, we go to Boislens. After that we pass by Nimporte, over the Forêt de Charbon to Siègecourt; then up to Le Recul and back by Princebourg, St. Guillaume, and Toutprès.

"As regards the observers, don't forget to use your field-glasses on the rolling stock; don't forget the precise direction of trains and motor transport; don't forget the railways and roads on every side; don't forget the canals; and for the Lord's and everybody else's sake, don't be surprised by Hun aircraft. As regards the pilots—keep in close formation when possible; don't straggle and don't climb above the proper height."

The pilots ran their engines once more, and the observers exchanged information about items such as Hun aerodromes and the number of railway stations at each large town. An air reconnaissance is essentially the observer's show; its main object being to supply the "I" people at headquarters with private bulletins from the back of the German front. The collection of reconnaissance reports is work of a highly skilled nature, or ought to be. Spying out the land is much more than a search of railways, roads, and the terrain generally. The experienced observer must know the German area over which he works rather better than he knows Salisbury Plain. The approximate position of railway junctions and stations, aerodromes, factories, and *depôts* should be familiar to him, so that he can without difficulty spot any new feature.

Also he must be something of a sleuth, particularly when using smoke as a clue. In the early morning a thin layer of smoke above a wood may mean a bivouac. If it be but a few miles behind the lines, it can evidence heavy artillery. A narrow stream of smoke near a railway will make an observer scan the line closely for a stationary train, as the Boche engine-drivers usually try to avoid detection by shutting off steam. The Hun has many other dodges to avoid publicity. When Allied aircraft appear, motor and horse transport remain immobile at the roadside or under trees. Artillery and infantry are packed under cover; though, for that matter, the enemy very rarely move troops in the daytime, preferring the night or early morning, when there are no troublesome eyes in the air.

To foil these attempts at concealment is the business of the observers who gather information for Army Headquarters and G. H.Q. For observers on corps work the detective problems are somewhat different. This department deals with hidden saps and battery positions, and draws and photographs conclusions from clues such as a muzzle-blast, fresh tracks, or an artificial cluster of trees. All reconnaissance observers must carry out a simultaneous search of the earth for movement and the sky for foes, and in addition keep their guns ready for instant use. And should anything happen to their machines, and a forced landing seem likely, they must sit tight and carry on so long as there is the slightest hope of a safe return.

A nos moutons. I made a long list in my note-book of the places where something useful was likely to be observed, and tried my gun by firing a few shots into the ground. We hung around, impatient at the long delay.

"Get into your machines," called the Squadron Commander at last, when a telephone message had reported that the weather conditions toward the east were no longer unfavourable. We took to the air and set off.

V. led his covey beyond Albert and well south of the Somme before he turned to the left. Then, with the strong wind behind us, we raced north-east and crossed the strip of trenches. The pilot of the emergency machine, which had come thus far to join the party if one of the other four dropped out, waved his hand in farewell and left for home.

Archie barked at us immediately, but he caused small trouble, as most of his attention was already claimed by a party of French machines half a mile ahead. Anyhow we should have shaken him off quickly, for at this stage of the journey, with a forty-mile wind reinforcing our usual air speed of about ninety-five miles an hour, our ground speed was sufficient to avoid lingering in any region made unhealthy by A.-A. guns. The water-marked ribbon of trenches seemed altogether puny and absurd during the few seconds when it was within sight. The winding Somme was dull and dirty as the desolation of its surrounding basin. Some four thousand feet above the ground a few clouds moved restlessly at the bidding of the wind.

Passing a few small woods, we arrived without interruption over the railway junction of Boislens. With arms free of the machine to avoid unnecessary vibration, the observers trained their glasses on the station and estimated the amount of rolling stock. A close search of the railway arteries only revealed one train. I grabbed pencil and notebook and wrote:

Boislens, 3.5 p.m. 6 R.S., 1 train going S.W.

Just west of our old friend Mossy-Face were two rows of flagrantly new trenches. As this is one of the points where the enemy made a stand after their 1917 spring retreat, it can be assumed that even as far back as last October they were preparing new lines of defence, Hindenburg or otherwise. Not far west of these defence works were two troublesome aerodromes at Bertincourt and Velu, both of which places have since been captured.

A hunt for an aerodrome followed. V., who knew the neighbourhood well, having passed above it some two-score times, was quick to spot a group of hitherto unnoted sheds north of Boislens, towards Mossy-Face. He circled over them to let me plot the pin-point position on the map and sketch the aerodrome and its surroundings. The Hun pilots, with thoughts of a possible bomb-raid, began to take their machines into the air for safety.

"Got 'em all?" Thus V., shouting through the rubber speaking-tube, one end of which was fixed inside my flying-cap, so that it always rested against my ear.

"Correct. Get on with the good work."

The good work led us over a region for ever associated with British arms. Some of the towns brought bitter memories of that anxious August three years back. Thus Nimporte, which saw a desperate but successful stand on one flank of the contemptible little army to gain time for the main body; Ventregris, scene of a cavalry charge that was a glorious tragedy; Làbas, where a battery of horse-gunners made for itself an imperishable name; Siègecourt, where the British might have retired into a trap but didn't; and Le Recul itself, whence they slipped away just in time.

In the station at Nimporte a train was waiting to move off, and two more were on their way to the military base of Plusprès. Both attempted to hide their heads by shutting off steam immediately the drone of our engines made itself heard; but we had spotted them from afar, and already they were noted for the information of Brass Hats.

The next item of interest was activity at a factory outside a little town. Black trails of smoke stretched away from the chimneys; and surely, as we approached a minute ago, a short column of lorries was passing along a road towards the factory. Yet when we reached the spot there was no sign of road transport. Nevertheless, I was certain I had seen some motor vehicles, and I entered the fact in my note-book. Likewise I took care to locate the factory site on my map, in case it deserved the honour of a bomb attack later.

Our bus led the way across the huge unwieldy Forêt de Charbon, patterned in rectangular fashion by intersecting roads, and we arrived at Siègecourt. This is at once a fortress and an industrial town. There are several railway stations around it, and these added greatly to the observers' collection of trains and trucks. The Huns below, with unpleasant memories of former visits from British aircraft, probably expected to be bombed. They threw up at us a large quantity of high-explosive shells, but the shots were all wide and we remained unworried. To judge by the quality of the A.-A. shooting each time I called there, it seemed likely that half-trained A.-A. gunners were allowed to cut their active service teeth on us at Siègecourt.

Having squeezed Siègecourt of all movement, we headed for Le Recul. Here the intricate patchwork of railway kept the observers busy, and six more trains were bagged. Then, as this was the farthest point east to be touched, we turned to the left and travelled homeward.

It was soon afterwards that our engine went dud. Instead of a rhythmic and continuous hum there was at regular intervals a break, caused by one of the cylinders missing explosion at each turn of the rotary engine. The rev.-counter showed that the number of revolutions per minute had fallen off appreciably. Decreased revs. meant less speed, and our only chance to keep with the others was to lose height continuously. We were then nearly fifty miles from the lines.

I noticed the gap in the engine's drone as soon as it began. An airman is accustomed to the full roar of his engine, and it never distracts his attention, any more than the noise of a waterfall distracts those who live near it. But if the roar becomes non-continuous and irregular he is acutely conscious of the sound.

When the machine began to lose height I knew there was a chronic miss. V. looked round and smiled reassuringly, though he himself was far from reassured. He tried an alteration in the carburettor mixture, but this did not remedy matters. Next, thinking that the engine might have been slightly choked, he cut off the petrol supply for a moment and put down the nose of the machine. The engine stopped, but picked up when the petrol was once more allowed to run. During the interval I thought the engine had ceased work altogether, and was about to stuff things into my pocket in readiness for a landing on hostile ground.

We continued in a westerly direction, with the one cylinder still cutting out. To make matters worse, the strong wind that had been our friend on the outward journey was now an enemy, for it was drifting us to the north, so that we were obliged to steer almost dead into it to follow the set course.

As we passed along the straight canal from Le Recul to Princebourg many barges were in evidence. Those at the side of the canal were taken to be moored up, and those in the middle to be moving, though the slowness of their speed made it impossible to decide on their direction, for from a height of ten thousand feet they seemed to be stationary. About a dozen Hun machines were rising from aero-dromes at Passementerie, away to the left, but if they were after us the attempt to reach our height in time was futile.

Between Le Recul and Princebourg we dropped fifteen hundred feet below the three rear machines, which hovered above us. Though I was far from feeling at home, it was necessary to sweep the sur-rounding country for transport of all kinds. This was done almost automatically, since I found myself unable to give a whole-hearted attention to the job, while the infernal motif of the engine's rag-time drone dominated everything and invited speculation on how much lower we were than the others, and whether we were likely to reach a friendly landing-ground. And all the while a troublesome verse chose very inopportunely to race across the background of my mind, in time with the engine, each cut-out being the end of a line. Once or twice I caught myself murmuring—

In that poor but honest 'ome,
Where 'er sorrowin' parints live,
They drink the shampyne wine she sends,
But never, never can fergive.

Slightly to the east of Princebourg, a new complication appeared in the shape of a small German machine. Seeing that our bus was in difficulties, it awaited an opportunity to pounce, and remained at a height slightly greater than ours, but some distance behind the bus that acted as rearguard to the party. Its speed must have been about ten miles an hour more than our own, for though the Hun pilot had probably throttled down, he was obliged to make his craft snake its way in short curves, so that it should not come within dangerous range of our guns. At times he varied this method by lifting the ma-chine almost to stalling point, letting her down again, and repeating the process. Once I saw some motor transport on a road. I leaned over the side to estimate their number, but gave up the task of doing so with accuracy under the double strain of watching the Hun scout and listening to the jerky voice of the engine.

As we continued to drop, the German evidently decided to finish us. He climbed a little and then rushed ahead. I fired at him in rapid bursts, but he kept to his course. He did not come near enough for a dive, however, as the rest of the party, two thousand feet above, had watched his movements, and as soon as he began to move nearer two of them fell towards him. Seeing that his game was spoiled the Boche went down steeply, and only flattened out when he was low enough to be safe from attack.

Near St Guillaume an anti-aircraft battery opened fire. The Hun pilot then thought it better to leave Archie to deal with us, and he annoyed us no more. Some of the shell-bursts were quite near, but we could not afford to lose height in distance-dodging, with our machine in a dubious condition twenty-five miles on the wrong side of the trenches.

Toutprès, to the south-west, was to have been included in the list of towns covered, but under the adverse circumstances V. decided not to battle against the wind more than was necessary to get us home. He therefore veered to the right, and steered due west. The south-west wind cut across and drifted us, so that our actual course was north-west. Our ground speed was now a good deal greater than if we had travelled directly west, and there was no extra distance to be covered, because of a large eastward bend in the lines as they wound north. We skirted the ragged Forêt de Quand-Même, and passed St Guillaume on our left.

The behaviour of the engine went from bad to worse, and the vibration became more and more intense. Once again I thought it would peter out before we were within gliding distance of British territory, and I therefore made ready to burn the machine—the last duty of an airman let in for the catastrophe of a landing among enemies. But the engine kept alive, obstinately and unevenly. V. held down the nose of the machine still farther, so as to gain the lines in the quickest possible time.

Soon we were treated to a display by the family ghost of the clan Archibald, otherwise an immense pillar of grey-white smoky substance that appeared very suddenly to windward of us. It stretched up vertically from the ground to a height about level with ours, which was then only five and a half thousand feet. We watched it curiously as it stood in an unbending rigidity similar to that of a giant waxwork, cold, unnatural, stupidly implacable, half unbelievable, and wholly ridiculous. At the top it sprayed round, like a stick of asparagus. For two or three months similar apparitions had been exhibited to us at rare intervals, nearly always in the same neighbourhood.

At first sight the pillars of smoke seemed not to disperse, but after an interval they apparently faded away as mysteriously as they had appeared. What was meant to be their particular branch of frightfulness I cannot say. One rumour was that they were an experiment in aerial gassing, and another that they were of some phosphorous compound. All I know is that they entertained us from time to time, with no apparent damage.

Archie quickly distracted our attention from the phantom pillar. We had been drifted to just south of Lille, possibly the hottest spot on the whole western front as regards anti-aircraft fire. Seeing one machine four to five thousand feet below its companions, the gunners very naturally concentrated on it. A spasmodic chorus of barking coughs drowned the almost equally spasmodic roar of the engine. V. dodged steeply and then raced, full out, for the lines. A sight of the dirty brown jig-saw of trenches heartened us greatly. A few minutes later we were within gliding distance of the British front. When we realised that even if the engine lost all life we could reach safety, nothing else seemed to matter, not even the storm of shell-bursts.

Suddenly the machine quivered, swung to the left, and nearly put itself in a flat spin. A large splinter of H.E. had sliced away part of the rudder. V. banked to prevent an uncontrolled side-slip, righted the bus as far as possible, and dived for the lines. These we passed at a great pace, but we did not shake off Archie until well on the right side, for at our low altitude the high-angle guns had a large radius of action that could include us. However, the menacing coughs finally ceased to annoy, and our immediate troubles were over.

The strain snapped, the air was an exhilarating tonic, the sun was warmly comforting, and everything seemed attractive, even the desolated jumble of waste ground below us. I opened a packet of chocolate and shared it with V., who was trying hard to fly evenly with an uneven rudder. I sang to him down the speaking-tube, but his nerves had stood enough for the day, and he wriggled the machine from one side to the other until I became silent. Contrariwise to the last, our engine recovered slightly now that its recovery was not so important, and it behaved well until it seized up for better or worse when we had landed.

From the aerodrome the pilots proceeded to tea and a bath, while we, the unfortunate observers, copied our notes into a detailed report, elaborated the sketches of the new aerodromes, and drove in our unkempt state to Headquarters, there to discuss the reconnaissance with spotlessly neat staff officers. At the end of the report one must give the height at which the job was done, and say whether the conditions were favourable or otherwise for observation. I thought of the absence of thick clouds or mist that might have made the work difficult. Then

I thought of the cylinder that missed and the chunk of rudder that was missing, but decided that these little inconveniences were unofficial. And the legend I felt in duty bound to write was: "Height 5,000–10,000 ft. Observation easy."

CHAPTER 5

There and Back

An inhuman philosopher or a strong, silent poseur might affect to treat with indifference his leave from the Front. Personally I have never met a philosopher inhuman enough or a poseur strongly silent enough to repress evidence of wild satisfaction, after several months of war at close quarters, on being given a railway warrant entitling him to ten days of England, home, and no duty. But if you are a normal soldier who dislikes fighting and detests discomfort, the date of your near-future holiday from the dreary scene of war will be one of the few problems that really matter.

Let us imagine a slump in great pushes at your sector of the line, since only during the interval of attack is the leave-list unpigeonholed. The weeks pass and your turn creeps close, while you pray that the lull may last until the day when, with a heavy haversack and a light heart, you set off to become a transient in Arcadia. The desire for a taste of freedom is sharpened by delay; but finally, after disappointment and postponement, the day arrives and you depart. Exchanging a "So long" with less fortunate members of the mess, you realise a vast difference in respective destinies. Tomorrow the others will be dodging crumps, archies, or official chits "for your information, please"; tomorrow, with luck, you will be dodging taxis in London.

During the journey you begin to cast out the oppressive feeling that a world and a half separates you from the pleasantly undisciplined life you once led. The tense influence of those twin bores of active service, routine and risk, gradually loosens hold, and your state of mind is tuned to a pitch half-way between the note of battle and that of a bank-holiday.

Yet a slight sense of remoteness lingers as you enter London. At first view the Charing Cross loiterers seem more foreign than the peasants of Picardy, the Strand and Piccadilly less familiar than the Albert-Pozières road. Not till a day or two later, when the remnants of strained pre-occupation with the big things of war have been charmed away by old haunts and old friends, do you feel wholly at home amid your rediscovered fellow-citizens, the Man in the Street, the Pacifist, the air-raid-funk Hysteric, the Lady Flag-Seller, the War Profiteer, the dear-boy Fluff Girl, the Prohibitionist, the England-for-the-Irish politician, the Conscientious Objector, the hotel-government bureaucrat, and other bulwarks of our united Empire. For the rest, you will want to cram into ten short days the average experiences of ten long weeks. If, like most of us, you are young and foolish, you will skim the bubbling froth of life and seek crowded diversion in the lighter follies, the passing shows, and *l'amour qui rit*. And you will probably return to the big things of war tired but mightily refreshed, and almost ready to welcome a further spell of routine and risk.

The one unsatisfactory aspect of leave from France, apart from its rarity, is the travelling. This, in a region congested by the more important traffic of war, is slow and burdensome to the impatient holiday-maker. Occasionally the Flying Corps officer is able to substitute an excursion by air for the land and water journey, if on one of the dates that sandwich his leave a bus of the type already flown by him must be chauffeured across the Channel. Such an opportunity is welcome, for besides avoiding discomfort, a joy-ride of this description often saves time enough to provide an extra day in England.

On the last occasion when I was let loose from the front on ticket-of-leave, I added twenty-four hours to my Blighty period by a chance meeting with a friendly ferry-pilot and a resultant trip as passenger in an aeroplane from a home *depôt*. Having covered the same route by train and boat a few days previously, a comparison between the two methods of travel left me an enthusiast for aerial transport in the golden age of after-the-war.

The leave train at Arrière was time-tabled for midnight, but as, under a war-time edict, French *cafés* and places where they lounge are closed at 10 p.m., it was at this hour that muddied officers and Tommies from every part of the Somme basin began to crowd the station.

Though confronted with a long period of waiting, in a packed entrance-hall that was only half-lit and contained five seats to be scrambled for by several hundred men, every one, projected beyond the immediate discomfort to the good time coming, seemed content.

The atmosphere of jolly expectancy was comparable to that of Waterloo Station on the morning of Derby Day. Scores of little groups gathered to talk the latest shop-talk from the trenches. A few of us who were acquainted with the corpulent and affable R.T.O.—it is part of an R.T.O.'s stock-in-trade to be corpulent and affable—sought out his private den, and exchanged yarns while commandeering his whisky. Stuff Redoubt had been stormed a few days previously, and a Canadian captain, who had been among the first to enter the Hun stronghold, told of the assault.

A sapper discussed some recent achievements of mining parties. A tired gunner subaltern spoke viciously of a stupendous bombardment that allowed little rest, less sleep, and no change of clothes. Time was overcome easily in thus looking at war along the varying angles of the infantryman, the gunner, the engineer, the machine-gun performer, and the flying officer, all fresh from their work.

The train, true to the custom of leave trains, was very late. When it did arrive, the good-natured jostling for seats again reminded one of the London to Epsom traffic of Derby Day. Somehow the crowd was squeezed into carriage accommodation barely sufficient for two-thirds of its number, and we left Arrière. Two French and ten British officers obtained a minimum of space in my compartment. We sorted out our legs, arms, and luggage, and tried to rest.

In my case sleep was ousted by thoughts of what was ahead. Ten days' freedom in England! The stout major on my left snored. The head of the hard-breathing Frenchman to the right slipped on to my shoulder. An unkempt subaltern opposite wriggled and turned in a vain attempt to find ease. I was damnably cramped, but above all impatient for the morrow. A passing train shrieked. Cold whiffs from the half-open window cut the close atmosphere. Slowly, and with frequent halts for the passage of war freights more urgent than ourselves, our train chugged northward. One hour, two hours, three hours of stuffy dimness and acute discomfort. Finally I sank into a troubled doze. When we were called outside Boulogne, I found my hand poised on the stout major's bald head, as if in benediction.

The soldier on leave, eager to be done with the preliminary journey, chafes at inevitable delay in Boulogne. Yet this largest of channel ports, in its present state, can show the casual passer-by much that is interesting. It has become almost a new town during the past three years. Formerly a headquarters of pleasure, a fishing centre and a principal port of call for Anglo-Continental travel, it has been transformed into an important military base. It is now wholly of the war; the armies absorb everything that it transfers from sea to railway, from human fuel for war's blast-furnace to the fish caught outside the harbour. The multitude of visitors from across the Channel is larger than ever; but instead of Paris, the Mediterranean, and the East, they are bound for less attractive destinations—the muddy battle-area and Kingdom Come.

The spirit of the place is altogether changed. From time immemorial Boulogne has included an English alloy in its French composition, but prior to the war it shared with other coastal resorts of France an outlook of smiling carelessness. Superficially it now seems more British than French, and, partly by reason of this, it impresses one as being severely business-like. The great number of khaki travellers is rivalled by a huge colony of khaki Base workers. Except for a few *matelots*, French fishermen, and the wharfside *cafés*, there is nothing to distinguish the quays from those of a British port.

The blue-bloused porters who formerly met one with volubility and the expectation of a fabulous tip have given place to khakied orderlies, the polite customs officials to old-soldier myrmidons of the worried embarkation officer. Store dumps with English markings are packed symmetrically on the cobbled stones. The transport lorries are all British, some of them still branded with the names of well-known London firms. Newly-built supply *depôts*, canteens, and military institutes fringe the town proper or rise behind the sand-ridges. One-time hotels and casinos along the sea-front between Boulogne and Wimereux have become hospitals, to which, by day and by night, the smooth-running motor ambulances bring broken soldiers. Other of the larger hotels, like the Folkestone and the Meurice, are now patronised almost exclusively by British officers.

The military note dominates everything. A walk through the main streets leaves an impression of mixed uniforms—bedraggled uniforms from trench and dugout, neat rainbow-tabbed uniforms worn by officers attached to the Base, graceful nursing uniforms, haphazard convalescent uniforms, discoloured blue uniforms of French *permissionaires*. Everybody is bilingual, speaking, if not both English and French, either one or other of these languages and the formless *Angliche patois* invented by Tommy and his hosts of the occupied zone. And everybody, soldier and civilian, treats as a matter of course the strange metamorphosis of what was formerly a haven for the gentle tourist.

The boat, due to steam off at eleven, left at noon,—a creditable performance as leave-boats go. On this occasion there was good reason for the delay, as we ceded the right of way to a hospital ship and waited while a procession of ambulance cars drove along the quay and unloaded their stretcher cases. The Red Cross vessel churned slowly out of the harbour, and we followed at a respectful distance.

Passengers on a Channel leave-boat are quieter than might be expected. With the country of war behind them they have attained the third degree of content, and so novel is this state after months of living on edge that the short crossing does not allow sufficient time for them to be moved to exuberance. One promenades the crowded deck happily, taking care not to tread on the staff spurs, and talks of fighting as if it were a thing of the half-forgotten past.

But there is no demonstration. In a well-known illustrated weekly a recent frontispiece, supposedly drawn "from material supplied," depicts a band of beaming Tommies, with weird water-bottles, haversacks, mess-tins, and whatnots dangling from their sheepskin coats, throwing caps and cheers high into the air as they greet the cliffs of England. As the subject of an Academy picture, or an illustration for *The Hero's Homecoming, or How a Bigamist Made Good*, the sketch would be excellent. But, except for the beaming faces, it is fanciful.

A shadowy view of the English coast-line draws a crowd to the starboard side of the boat, whence one gazes long and joyfully at the dainty cliffs. Yet there is no outward sign of excitement; the deep satisfaction felt by all is of too intimate a nature to call for cheering and cap-throwing. The starboard deck remains crowded as the shore looms larger, and until, on entry into Dovstone harbour, one prepares for disembarkation.

The Front seemed very remote from the train that carried us from Dovstone to London. How could one think of the wilderness with the bright hop-fields of Kent chasing past the windows? Then came the mass-meeting of brick houses that skirt London, and finally the tunnel which is the approach to the terminus. As the wheels rumbled through the darkness of it they suggested some lines of stray verse beginning—

Twenty to eleven by all the clocks of Piccadilly;
Buy your love a lily-bloom, buy your love a rose.

It had been raining, and the faint yet unmistakable tang sniffed from wet London streets made one feel at home more than anything else. We dispersed, each to make his interval of heaven according to taste, means, and circumstances. That same evening I was fortunate in being helped to forget the realities of war by two experiences. A much-moustached A.P.M. threatened me with divers penalties for the wearing of a soft hat; and I was present at a merry gathering of theatrical luminaries, enormously interested in themselves, but enormously bored by the war, which usurped so much newspaper space that belonged by rights to the lighter drama.

Curtain and interval of ten days, at the end of which I was offered a place as passenger in a machine destined for my own squadron. The bus was to be taken to an aircraft *depôt* in France from Rafborough Aerodrome. Rafborough is a small town galvanised into importance by its association with flying. Years ago, in the far-away days when aviation itself was matter for wonder, the pioneers who concerned themselves with the possibilities of war flying made their headquarters at Rafborough.

An experimental factory, rich in theory, was established, and near it was laid out an aerodrome for the more practical work. Thousands of machines have since been tested on the rough-grassed aerodrome, while the neighbouring Royal Aircraft Factory has continued to produce designs, ideas, aeroplanes, engines, and aircraft accessories. Formerly most types of new machines were put through their official paces at Rafborough, and most types, including some captures from the Huns, were to be seen in its sheds. Probably Rafborough has harboured a larger variety of aircraft and aircraft experts than any other place in the world.

My friend the ferry-pilot having announced that the carriage waited, I strapped our baggage, some new gramophone records, and myself into the observer's office. I also took—tell this not in Gath, for the transport of dogs by aeroplane has been forbidden—a terrier pup sent to a fellow-officer by his family. At first the puppy was on a cord attached to some bracing-wires; but as he showed fright when the machine took off from the ground, I kept him on my lap for a time. Here he remained subdued and apparently uninterested. Later, becoming inured to the engine's drone and the slight vibration, he roused himself and wanted to explore the narrowing passage toward the tail-end of the fuselage. The little chap was, however, distinctly pleased to be on land again at Saint Gregoire, where he kept well away from the machine, as if uncertain whether the strange giant of an animal were friendly or a dog-eater.

It was a morning lovely enough to be that of the world's birthday.

Not a cloud flecked the sky, the flawless blue of which was made tenuous by sunlight. The sun brightened the kaleidoscopic earthscape below us, so that rivers and canals looked like quicksilver threads, and even the railway lines glistened. The summer countryside, as viewed from an aeroplane, is to my mind the finest scene in the world—an unexampled scene, of which poets will sing in the coming days of universal flight. The varying browns and greens of the field-pattern merge into one another delicately; the woods, splashes of bottle-green, relieve the patchwork of hedge from too ordered a scheme; rivers and roads criss-cross in riotous manner over the vast tapestry; pleasant villages and farm buildings snuggle in the valleys or straggle on the slopes.

The wide and changing perspective is full of a harmony unspoiled by the jarring notes evident on solid ground. Ugliness and dirt are camouflaged by the clean top of everything. Grimy towns and jerry-built suburbs seem almost attractive when seen in mass from a height. Slums, the dead uniformity of long rows of houses, sordid back-gardens, bourgeois public statues—all these eyesores are mercifully hidden by the roofed surface. The very factory chimneys have a certain air of impressiveness, in common with church towers and the higher buildings. Once, on flying over the pottery town of Coalport—the most uninviting place I have ever visited—I found that the altered perspective made it look delightful.

A westward course, with the fringe of London away on our left, brought us to the coast-line all too soon. Passing Dovstone, the bus continued across the Channel. A few ships, tiny and slow-moving when observed from a machine at 8000 feet and travelling 100 miles an hour, spotted the sea. A cluster of what were probably destroyers threw out trails of dark smoke. From above mid-Channel we could see plainly the two coasts—that of England knotted into small creeks and capes, that of France bent into large curves, except for the sharp corner at Grisnez. Behind was Blighty, with its greatness and its— sawdust. Ahead was the province of battle, with its good-fellowship and its—mud. I lifted the puppy to show him his new country, but he merely exhibited boredom and a dislike of the sudden rush of air.

From Cape Grisnez we steered north-east towards Calais, so as to have a clearly defined course to the aircraft depôt of Saint Gregoire. After a cross-Channel flight one notes a marked difference between the French and English earthscapes. The French towns and villages seem to sprawl less than those of England, and the countryside in general is more compact and regular. The roads are straight and tree-bordered, so that they form almost as good a guide to an airman as the railways. In England the roads twist and twirl through each other like the threads of a spider's web, and failing rail or river or prominent landmarks, one usually steers by compass rather than trust to roads.

At Calais we turned to the right and followed a network of canals south-westward to Saint Gregoire, where was an aircraft *depôt* similar to the one at Rafborough. New machines call at Saint Gregoire before passing to the service of aerodromes, and in its workshops machines damaged but repairable are made fit for further service. It is also a higher training centre for airmen. Before they join a squadron pilots fresh from their instruction in England gain experience on service machines belonging to the "pool" at Saint Gregoire.

Having been told by telephone from my squadron that one of our pilots had been detailed to take the recently arrived bus to the Somme, I awaited his arrival and passed the time to good purpose in watching the aerobatics and sham fights of the pool pupils. Every now and then another plane from England would arrive high over the aerodrome, spiral down and land into the wind. The ferry-pilot who had brought me left for Rafborough almost immediately on a much-flown "quirk." The machine he had delivered at Saint Gregoire was handed over to a pilot from *Umpty* Squadron when the latter reported, and we took to the air soon after lunch. The puppy travelled by road over the last lap of his long journey, in the company of a lorry driver.

The bus headed east while climbing, for we had decided to follow the British lines as far as the Somme, a course which would be prolific in interesting sights, and which would make us eligible for that rare gift of the gods, an air-fight over friendly territory.

The coloured panorama below gave place gradually to a wilderness—ugly brown and pock-marked. The roads became bare and dented, the fields were mottled by shell-holes, the woods looked like scraggy patches of burnt furze. It was a district of great deeds and glorious deaths—the desolation surrounding the Fronts of yesterday and today.

North of Ypres we turned to the right and hovered awhile over this city of ghosts. Seen from above, the shell of the ancient city suggests a grim reflection on the mutability of beauty. I sought a comparison, and could think of nothing but the skeleton of a once charming woman. The ruins stood out in a magnificent disorder that was starkly impressive. Walls without roof, buildings with two sides, churches without tower, were everywhere prominent, as though proud to survive the orgy of destruction. The shattered Cathedral retained much of its former grandeur. Only the old Cloth Hall, half-razed and without arch or belfry, seemed to cry for vengeance on the vandalism that wrecked it. The gaping skeleton was grey-white, as if sprinkled by the powder of decay. And one fancies that at night-time the ghosts of 1915 mingle with the ghosts of Philip of Spain's era of conquest and the ghosts of great days in other centuries, as they search the ruins for relics of the city they knew.

Left of us was the salient, studded with broken villages that became household names during the two epic Battles of Ypres. The brown soil was dirty, shell-ploughed, and altogether unlovely. Those strange markings, which from our height looked like the tortuous pathways of a serpent, were the trenches, old and new, front-line, support, and communication. Small saps projected from the long lines at every angle. So complicated was the jumble that the sinister region of No Man's Land, with its shell-holes, dead bodies, and barbed wire, was scarcely distinguishable.

A brown strip enclosed the trenches and wound northward and southward. Its surface had been torn and battered by innumerable shells. On its fringe, among the copses and crests, were the guns, though these were evidenced only by an occasional flash. Behind, in front, and around them were those links in the chain of war, the oft-cut telephone wires. The desolation seemed utterly bare, though one knew that over and under it, hidden from eyes in the air, swarmed the slaves of the gun, the rifle, and the bomb.

Following the belt of wilderness southward, we were obliged to veer to the right at St. Eloi, so as to round a sharp bend. Below the bend, and on the wrong side of it, was the Messines Ridge, the recent capture of which has straightened the line as far as Hooge, and flattened the Ypres salient out of existence as a salient. Next came the torn and desolate outline of Plug Street Wood, and with it reminiscences of a splendid struggle against odds when shell-shortage hampered our 1915 armies. Armentières appeared still worthy to be called a town. It was battered, but much less so than Ypres, possibly because it was a hotbed of German espionage until last year. The triangular denseness of Lille loomed up from the flat soil on our left.

As we passed down the line the brown band narrowed until it seemed a strip of discoloured water-marked ribbon sewn over the mosaic of open country. The trench-lines were monotonous in their sameness. The shell-spotted area bulged at places, as for example Festubert, Neuve Chapelle (of bitter memory), Givenchy, Hulluch, and Loos. Lens, well behind the German trenches in those days, showed few marks of bombardment. The ribbon of ugliness widened again between Souchez and the yet uncaptured Vimy Ridge, but afterwards contracted as far as Arras, that ragged sentinel of the war frontier.

At Arras we entered our own particular province, which, after months of flying over it, I knew better than my native county. Gun-flashes became numerous, kite balloons hung motionless, and we met restless aeroplane formations engaged on defensive patrols. With these latter on guard our chance of a scrap with roving enemy craft would have been remote; though for that matter neither we nor they saw a single black-crossed machine throughout the afternoon.

From Gommecourt to the Somme was an area of concentrated destruction. The wilderness swelled outwards, becoming twelve miles wide at parts. Tens of thousands of shells had pocked the dirty soil, scores of mine explosions had cratered it. Only the pen of a Zola could describe adequately the zone's intense desolation, as seen from the air. Those ruins, suggestive of abandoned scrap-heaps, were formerly villages. They had been made familiar to the world through matter-of-fact reports of attack and counter-attack, capture and re-capture. Each had a tale to tell of systematic bombardment, of crumbling walls, of wild hand-to-hand fighting, of sudden evacuation and occupation. Now they were nothing but useless piles of brick and glorious names—Thiepval, Pozières, La Boiselle, Guillemont, Flers, Hardecourt, Guinchy, Combles, Bouchavesnes, and a dozen others.

Of all the crumbled roads the most striking was the long, straight one joining Albert and Bapaume. It looked fairly regular for the most part, except where the trenches cut it. Beyond the scrap-heap that once was Pozières two enormous quarries dipped into the earth on either side of the road. Until the Messines explosion they were the largest mine craters on the western front. Farther along the road was the scene of the first tank raids, where on September 16 the metal monsters waddled across to the gaping enemy and ate up his pet machine-gun emplacements before he had time to recover from his surprise.

At the road's end was the forlorn stronghold of Bapaume. One by one the lines of defence before it had been stormed, and it was obvious that the town must fall, though its capture was delayed until months later by a fierce defence at the Butte de Warlencourt and elsewhere. The advance towards Bapaume was of special interest to R.F.C. squadrons on the Somme, for the town had been a troublesome centre of anti-aircraft devilries. Our field-guns now being too close for Herr Archie, he had moved to more comfortable headquarters.

Some eight miles east of Bapaume the Bois d'Havrincourt stood out noticeably. Around old Mossy-Face, as the wood was known in R.F.C. messes, were clustered many Boche aerodromes. Innumerable duels had been fought in the air-country between Mossy-Face and the lines. Every fine day the dwellers in the trenches before Bapaume saw machines swerving round each other in determined effort to destroy. This region was the hunting-ground of many dead notabilities of the air, including the Fokker stars Boelcke and Immelmann, besides British pilots as brilliant but less advertised.

Below the Pozières-Bapaume road were five small woods, grouped like the Great Bear constellation of stars. Their roots were feeding on hundreds of dead bodies, after each of the five—Trones, Mametz, Foureaux, Delville, and Bouleaux—had seen wild encounters with bomb and bayonet beneath its dead trees. Almost in the same position relative to the cluster of woods as is the North Star to the Great Bear, was a scrap-heap larger than most, amid a few walls yet upright. This was all that remained of the fortress of Combles. For two years the enemy strengthened it by every means known to military science, after which the British and French rushed in from opposite sides and met in the main street.

A few minutes down the line brought our machine to the sparkling Somme, the white town of Péronne, and the then junction of the British and French lines. We turned north-west and made for home. Passing over some lazy sausage balloons, we reached Albert. Freed at last from the intermittent shelling from which it suffered for so long, the town was picking up the threads of activity. The sidings were full of trucks, and a procession of some twenty lorries moved slowly up the road to Bouzincourt. As reminder of anxious days, we noted a few skeleton roofs, and the giant Virgin Mary in tarnished gilt, who, after withstanding bombardments sufficient to have wrecked a cathedral, leaned over at right angles to her pedestal, suspended in apparently miraculous fashion by the three remaining girders.

We flew once more over a countryside of multi-coloured crops and fantastic woods, and so to the aerodrome.

★ ★ ★ ★ ★ ★ ★ ★ ★

Snatches of familiar flying-talk, unheard during the past ten days of leave, floated from the tea-table as I entered the mess:

"Folded up as he pulled out of the dive—weak factor of safety—side-slipped away from Archie—vertical gust—choked on the fine adjustment—made rings round the Hun—went down in flames near Douai."

The machine that "went down in flames near Douai" was piloted by the man whose puppy I had brought from England.

A Cloud Reconnaissance

Clouds, say the text-books of meteorology, are collections of partly condensed water vapour or of fine ice crystals. Clouds, mentioned in terms of the newspaper and the club, are dingy masses of nebulousness under which the dubious politician, company promoter, or other merchant of hot air is hidden from open attack and exposure. Clouds, to the flying officer on active service, are either useful friends or unstrafeable enemies. The hostile clouds are very high and of the ice-crystal variety. They form a light background, against which aeroplanes are boldly silhouetted, to the great advantage of anti-aircraft gunners. The friendly or water-vapour clouds are to be found several thousands of feet lower. If a pilot be above them they help him to dodge writs for trespass, which Archibald the bailiff seeks to hand him. When numerous enough to make attempts at observation ineffective, they perform an even greater service for him—that of arranging for a day's holiday. And at times the R.F.C. pilot, like the man with a murky past, is constrained to have clouds for a covering against attack; as you shall see if you will accompany me on the trip about to be described.

★ ★ ★ ★ ★ ★ ★ ★

The period is the latter half of September, 1916, a time of great doings on the Somme front. After a few weeks of comparative inaction—if methodical consolidation and intense artillery preparation can be called inaction—the British are once more denting the Boche line. Flers, Martinpuich, Courcelette, and Eaucourt l'Abbaye have fallen within the past week, and the tanks have made their first ungainly bow before the curtain of war, with the superlatives of the war correspondent in close attendance. Leave from France has been cancelled indefinitely.

Our orders are to carry through all the reconnaissance work allotted to us, even though weather conditions place such duties near the border-line of possible accomplishment. That is why we now propose to leave the aerodrome, despite a great lake of cloud that only allows the sky to be seen through rare gaps, and a sixty-mile wind that will fight us on the outward journey. Under these circumstances we shall probably find no friendly craft east of the trenches, and, as a consequence, whatever Hun machines are in the air will be free to deal with our party. However, since six machines are detailed for the job, I console myself with the old tag about safety in numbers.

We rise to a height of 3000 feet, and rendezvous there. From the flight-commander's bus I look back to see how the formation is shaping, and discover that we number but five, one machine having failed to start by reason of a dud engine. We circle the aerodrome, waiting for a sixth bus, but nobody is sent to join us. The "Carry on" signal shows up from the ground, and we head eastward.

After climbing another fifteen hundred feet, we enter the clouds. It is now impossible to see more than a yard or two through the intangible wisps of grey-white vapour that seem to float around us, so that our formation loses its symmetry, and we become scattered. Arrived in the clear atmosphere above the clouds my pilot throttles down until the rear machines have appeared and re-formed. We then continue in the direction of the trenches, with deep blue infinity above and the unwieldy cloud-banks below. Familiar landmarks show up from time to time through holes in the white screen.

Against the violent wind, far stronger than we found it near the ground, we make laboured progress. Evidently, two of the formation are in difficulties, for they drop farther and farther behind. Soon one gives in and turns back, the pilot being unable to maintain pressure for his petrol supply. I shout the news through the speaking-tube, and hear, in reply from the flight-commander, a muffled comment, which might be "Well!" but it is more likely to be something else. Three minutes later the second bus in trouble turns tail. Its engine has been missing on one cylinder since the start, and is not in a fit state for a trip over enemy country.

Again I call to the leader, and again hear a word ending in "ell." The two remaining machines close up, and we continue. Very suddenly one of them drops out, with a rocker-arm gone. Its nose goes down, and it glides into the clouds. Yet again I call the flight-commander's attention to our dwindling numbers, and this time I cannot mistake the single-syllabled reply. It is a full-throated "Hell!"

For my part I compare the party to the ten little nigger boys, and wonder when the only survivor, apart from our own machine, will leave. I look towards it anxiously. The wings on one side are much lighter than those on the other, and I therefore recognise it as the Tripehound's bus. There is ground for misgiving, for on several occasions during the past ten minutes it has seemed to fly in an erratic manner. The cause of this, as we find out on our return, is that for five minutes the Tripehound has been leaning over the side, with the joystick held between his knees while attempting to fasten a small door in the cowling round the engine, left open by a careless mechanic. It is important to shut the opening, as otherwise the wind may rush inside and tear off the cowling. Just as a short band of the trench line south of Arras can be seen through a gap, the Tripehound, having found that he cannot possibly reach far enough to close the protruding door, signals that he must go home.

I do not feel altogether sorry to see our last companion leave, as we have often been told not to cross the lines on a reconnaissance flight with less than three machines; and with the wind and the low clouds, which now form an opaque window, perforated here and there by small holes, a long observation journey over Bocheland by a single aeroplane does not seem worthwhile. But the flight-commander, remembering the recent order about completing a reconnaissance at all costs, thinks differently and decides to go on. To get our bearings he holds down the nose of the machine until we have descended beneath the clouds, and into full view of the open country.

We find ourselves a mile or two beyond Arras. As soon as the bus appears it is bracketed in front, behind, and on both sides by black shell-bursts. We swerve aside, but more shells quickly follow. The shooting is particularly good, for the Archie people have the exact range of the low clouds slightly above us. Three times we hear the hiss of flying fragments of high explosive, and the lower left plane is unevenly punctured. We lose height for a second to gather speed, and then, to my relief, the pilot zooms up to a cloud. Although the gunners can no longer see their target, they loose off a few more rounds and trust to luck that a stray shell may find us. These bursts are mostly far wide of the mark, although two of them make ugly black blotches against the whiteness of the vapour through which we are rising.

Once more we emerge into the open space between sky and cloud. The flight-commander takes the mouthpiece of his telephone tube and shouts to me that he intends completing the round above the clouds. To let me search for railway and other traffic he will descend into view of the ground at the most important points. He now sets a compass course for Toutprès, the first large town of the reconnaissance, while I search all around for possible enemies. At present the sky is clear, but at any minute enemy police craft may appear from the unbroken blue or rise through the clouds.

The slowness of our ground speed, due to the fierce wind, allows me plenty of time to admire the strangely beautiful surroundings. Above is the inverted bowl of blue, bright for the most part, but duller towards the horizon-rim. The sun pours down a vivid light, which spreads quicksilver iridescence over the cloud-tops. Below is the cloud-scape, fantastic and far-stretching. The shadow of our machine is surrounded by a halo of sunshine as it darts along the irregular white surface. The clouds dip, climb, twist, and flatten into every conceivable shape. Thrown together as they never could be on solid earth are outlines of the wildest and tamest features of a world unspoiled by battlefield, brick towns, ruins, or other ulcers on the face of nature.

Jagged mountains, forests, dainty hills, waterfalls, heavy seas, plateaux, precipices, quiet lakes, rolling plains, caverns, chasms, and dead deserts merge into one another, all in a uniform white, as though wrapped in cotton wool and laid out for inspection in haphazard continuity. And yet, for all its mad irregularity, the cloud-scape from above is perfectly harmonious and never tiring. One wants to land on the clean surface and explore the jungled continent. Sometimes, when passing a high projection, the impulse comes to lean over and grab a handful of the fleecy covering.

After being shut off from the ground for a quarter of an hour, we are able to look down through a large chasm. Two parallel canals cut across it, and these we take to be part of the canal junction below Toutprès. This agrees with our estimate of speed, wind, and time, according to which we should be near the town. The pilot takes the machine through the clouds, and we descend a few hundred feet below them.

To disconcert Archie we travel in zigzags, while I search for items of interest. A train is moving south, and another is entering Toutprès from the east. A few barges are dotted among the various canals. Bordering a wood to the west is an aerodrome. About a dozen aeroplanes are in line on the ground, but the air above it is empty of Boche craft.

Evidently the Huns below had not expected a visit from hostile machines on such a day, for Archie allows several minutes to pass before introducing himself. A black puff then appears on our level some distance ahead. We change direction, but the gunners find our new position and send bursts all round the bus. The single *wouff* of the first shot has become a jerky chorus that swells or dwindles according to the number of shells and their nearness.

I signal to the flight-commander that I have finished with Tout-près, whereupon we climb into the clouds and comparative safety. We rise above the white intangibility and steer north-east, in the direction of Passementerie. I continue to look for possible aggressors. The necessity for a careful look-out is shown when a group of black specks appears away to the south, some fifteen hundred feet above us. In this area and under today's weather conditions, the odds are a hundred to one that they will prove to be Boches.

We lose height until our bus is on the fringe of the clouds and ready to escape out of sight. Apparently the newcomers do not spot us in the first place, for they are flying transverse to our line of flight. A few minutes later they make the discovery, turn in our direction, and begin a concerted dive. All this while I have kept my field-glasses trained on them, and as one machine turns I can see the Maltese crosses painted on the wings. The question of the strangers' nationality being answered, we slip into a cloud to avoid attack.

The flight-commander thinks it advisable to remain hidden by keeping inside the clouds. He must therefore steer entirely by compass, without sun or landmark to guide him. As we leave the clear air a left movement of the rudder, without corresponding bank, swings the machine to the north, so that its nose points away from the desired course. The pilot puts on a fraction of right rudder to counteract the deviation. We veer eastward, but rather too much, if the swaying needle of the compass is to be believed. A little left rudder again puts the needle into an anti-clockwise motion. With his attention concentrated on our direction, the pilot, impatient at waiting for the needle to become steady, unconsciously kicks the rudder-controls, first to one side, then to the other. The needle begins to swing around, and the compass is thus rendered useless for the time being. For the next minute or two, until it is safe to leave the clouds, the pilot must now keep the machine straight by instinct, and trust to his sense of direction.

A similar mishap often happens when flying through cloud. Pilots have been known to declare that all compasses are liable to swing of their own accord when in clouds, though the real explanation is probably that they themselves have disturbed the needle unduly by a continuous pressure on each side of the rudder-bar in turn, thus causing an oscillation of the rudder and a consequent zigzagged line of flight. The trouble is more serious than it would seem to the layman, as when the compass is out of action, and no other guides are available, one tends to drift round in a large circle, like a man lost in the jungle. Should the craft be driven by a rotary engine, the torque, or outward wash from the propeller, may make a machine edge more and more to the left, unless the pilot is careful to allow for this tendency.

Such a drift to the left has taken us well to the north of a straight line between Toutprès and Passementerie, as we discover on leaving the clouds for a second or two, so as to correct the error with the aid of landmarks. But the compass has again settled down to good behaviour, and we are able to get a true course before we climb back to the sheltering whiteness.

A flight inside the clouds is far from pleasant. We are hemmed in by a drifting formlessness that looks like thin steam, but, unlike steam, imparts a sensation of coldness and clamminess. The eye cannot penetrate farther than about a yard beyond the wing tips. Nothing is to be seen but the aeroplane, nothing is to be heard but the droning hum of the engine, which seems louder than ever amid the isolation.

I am bored, cold, and uncomfortable. Time drags along lamely; five minutes masquerade as half an hour, and only by repeated glances at the watch do I convince myself that we cannot yet have reached the next objective. I study the map for no particular reason except that it is something to do. Then I decide that the Lewis gun ought to be fired as a test whether the working parts are still in good order. I hold the spade-grip, swing round the circular mounting until the gun points to the side, and loose five rounds into the unpleasant vapour. The flight-commander, startled at the sudden clatter, turns round. Finding that the fire was mine and not an enemy's, he shakes his fist as a protest against the sudden disturbance. Even this action is welcome, as being evidence of companionship.

When the pilot, judging that Passementerie should be below, takes the machine under the clouds, I feel an immense relief, even though the exit is certain to make us a target for Archie. We emerge slightly to the west of the town. There is little to be observed; the railways are bare of trains, and the station contains only an average number of trucks. Four black-crossed aeroplanes are flying over their aerodrome at a height of some two thousand feet. Three of them begin to climb, perhaps in an attempt to intercept us. However, our bus has plenty of time to disappear, and this we do quickly—so quickly that the A.-A. batteries have only worried us to the extent of half a dozen shells, all wide of the mark.

We rise right through the white screen into full view of the sun. Apparently the sky is clear of intruders, so we turn for three-quarters of a circle and head for Plusprès, the third point of call. The wind now being behind the machine in a diagonal direction, our speed in relation to the ground is twice the speed of the outward half of the journey. The sun is pleasantly warming, and I look towards it gratefully. A few small marks, which may or may not be sun-spots, flicker across its face. To get an easier view I draw my goggles, the smoke-tinted glasses of which allow me to look at the glare without blinking. In a few seconds I am able to recognise the spots as distant aeroplanes moving in our direction. Probably they are the formation that we encountered on the way to Passementerie.

Their object in keeping between us and the sun is to remain unobserved with the help of the blinding stream of light, which throws a haze around them. I call the pilot's attention to the scouts, and yet again we fade into the clouds. This time, with the sixty-mile wind as our friend, there is no need to remain hidden for long. Quite soon we shall have to descend to look at Plusprès, the most dangerous point on the round.

When we take another look at earth I find that the pilot has been exact in timing our arrival at the important Boche base—too exact, indeed, for we find ourselves directly over the centre of the town. Only somebody who has been Archied from Plusprès can realise what it means to fly right over the stronghold at four thousand feet. The advanced lines of communication that stretch westward to the Arras-Péronne front all hinge on Plusprès, and for this reason it often shows activity of interest to the aeroplane observer and his masters. The Germans are therefore highly annoyed when British aircraft arrive on a tour of inspection. To voice their indignation they have concentrated many anti-aircraft guns around the town. What is worse, the Archie fire at Plusprès is more accurate than at any other point away from the actual front, as witness the close bracket formed by the sighting shots that greet our solitary bus.

From a hasty glance at the station and railway lines, while we slip away to another level, I gather that many trains and much rolling stock are to be bagged. The work will have to be done under serious difficulties in the shape of beastly black bursts and the repeated changes of direction necessary to dodge them. We bank sharply, side-slip, lose height, regain it, and perform other erratic evolutions likely to spoil the gunners' aim; but the area is so closely sprinkled by shells that, to whatever point the machine swerves, we always hear the menacing report of bursting H.E.

It is no easy matter to observe accurately while in my present condition of "wind up," created by the coughing of Archie. I lean over to count the stationary trucks in the sidings. "*Wouff, wouff, wouff,*" interrupts Archie from a spot deafeningly near; and I withdraw into "the office," otherwise the observer's cockpit. Follows a short lull, during which I make another attempt to count the abnormal amount of rolling stock. "*Wouff—Hs—sss!*" shrieks another shell, as it throws a large H.E. splinter past our tail. Again I put my head in the office. I write down an approximate estimate of the number of trucks, and no longer attempt to sort them out, so many to a potential train. A hunt over the railway system reveals no fewer than twelve trains. These I pencil-point on my map, as far as I am able to locate them.

A massed collection of vehicles remain stationary in what must be either a large square or the market-place. I attempt to count them, but am stopped by a report louder than any of the preceding ones. Next instant I find myself pressed tightly against the seat. The whole of the machine is lifted about a hundred feet by the compression from a shell that has exploded a few yards beneath our undercarriage. I begin to wonder whether all our troubles have been swept away by a direct hit; but an examination of the machine shows no damage beyond a couple of rents in the fabric of the fuselage. That finishes my observation work for the moment. Not with a court-martial as the only alternative could I carry on the job until we have left Archie's inferno of frightfulness. The flight-commander is of the same mind, and we nose into the clouds, pursued to the last by the insistent smoke-puffs.

When the bus is once again flying between sky and cloud, we begin to feel more at home. No other craft come within range of vision, so that without interruption we reach Aucoin, the fourth railway junction to be spied upon. The rolling stock there is scarcely enough for two train-loads, and no active trains can be spotted. We hover above the town for a minute, and then leave for Boislens.

The machine now points westward and homeward, and thus has

the full benefit of the wind, which accelerates our ground speed to about a hundred and fifty miles an hour. The gods take it into their heads to be kind, for we are not obliged to descend through the clouds over Boislens, as the region can be seen plainly through a gap large enough to let me count the R.S. and note that a train, with steam up, stands in the station.

As Boislens is the last town mentioned by the H.Q. people who mapped out the reconnaissance, the job is all but completed. Yet twelve miles still separate us from the nearest bend of the trench line, and a twelve-mile area contains plenty of room for a fight. Since the open atmosphere shows no warning of an attack, I look closely toward the sun—for a fast scout will often try to surprise a two-seater by approaching between its quarry and the sun.

At first I am conscious of nothing but a strong glare; but when my goggled eyes become accustomed to the brightness, I see, or imagine I see, an indistinct oblong object surrounded by haze. I turn away for a second to avoid the oppressive light. On seeking the sun again I find the faint oblong more pronounced. For one instant it deviates from the straight line between our bus and the sun, and I then recognise it as an aeroplane. I also discover that a second machine is hovering two thousand feet above the first.

The chief hobby of the flight-commander is to seek a scrap. Immediately I make known to him the presence of hostile craft he tests his gun in readiness for a fight. Knowing by experience that if he starts manoeuvring round a Hun he will not break away while there is the slightest chance of a victory, I remind him, by means of a note-book leaf, that since our job is a reconnaissance, the R.F.C. law is to return quickly with our more or less valuable information, and to abstain from such luxuries as unnecessary fights, unless a chance can be seized over British ground. Although he does not seem too pleased at the reminder he puts down the nose of the machine, so as to cross the lines in the shortest possible time.

The first Hun scout continues the dive to within three hundred yards, at which range I fire a few short bursts, by way of an announcement to the Boche that we are ready for him and protected from the rear. He flattens out and sits behind our tail at a respectful distance, until the second scout has joined him. The two separate and prepare to swoop down one from each side.

But we are now passing the trenches, and just as one of our attackers begins to dive, a formation of de Havilands (British pusher scouts) arrives to investigate. The second Boche plants himself between us and the newcomers, while his companion continues to near until he is a hundred and fifty yards from us. At this range I rattle through the rest of the ammunition drum, and the Hun swerves aside. We now recognise the machine as an Albatross scout or "German spad," a most successful type that only entered the lists a fortnight beforehand. Finding that they have to reckon with five de Havilands, the two Huns turn sharply and race eastward, their superior speed saving them from pursuit.

We pass through the clouds for the last time on the trip, and fly home very soberly, while I piece together my hurried notes. The Squadron Commander meets us in the aerodrome with congratulations and a desire for information.

"Seen anything?" he asks.

"Fourteen trains and some M. T.," I reply.

"And a few thousand clouds," adds the flight-commander.

By the time I have returned from the delivery of my report at G.H.Q., the wing office has sent orders that we are to receive a mild censure for carrying out a reconnaissance with only one machine. The Squadron Commander grins as he delivers the reproof, so that we do not feel altogether crushed.

"Don't do it again," he concludes.

As we have not the least desire to do it again, the order is likely to be obeyed.

CHAPTER 7

Ends and Odds

As a highly irresponsible prophet I am convinced that towards the end of the war hostilities in the air will become as decisive as hostilities on land or sea. An obvious corollary is that the how and when of peace's coming must be greatly influenced by the respective progress, during the next two years, of the belligerents' flying services.

This view is far less fantastic than the whirlwind development of war-flying witnessed by all of us since 1914. Indeed, to anybody with a little imagination and some knowledge of what is in preparation among the designers and inventors of various countries, that statement would seem more self-evident than extreme. Even the average spectator of aeronautical advance in the past three years must see that if anything like the same rate of growth be maintained, by the end of 1918 aircraft numbered in tens of thousands and with extraordinary capacities for speed, climb, and attack will make life a burden to ground troops, compromise lines of communication, cause repeated havoc to factories and strongholds, and promote loss of balance among whatever civilian populations come within range of their activity.

To emphasise the startling nature of aeronautical expansion—past, present, and future—let us trace briefly the progress of the British Flying Corps from pre-war conditions to their present state of high efficiency. When the Haldane-Asquith brotherhood were caught napping, the Flying Corps possessed a seventy odd (very odd) aeroplanes, engined by the unreliable Gnome and the low-powered Renault. Fortunately it also possessed some very able officers, and these succeeded at the outset in making good use of doubtful material. One result of the necessary reconstruction was that a large section of the original corps seceded to the Navy and the remainder came under direct control of the Army. The Royal Naval Air Service began to specialise in bomb raids, while the Royal Flying Corps (Military Wing) sent whatever machines it could lay hands on to join the old contemptibles in France. Both services proceeded to increase in size and importance at break-neck speed.

The rapid expansion of the R.N.A.S. allowed for a heavy surplus of men and machines beyond the supply necessary for the purely naval branch of the service. From this force a number of squadrons went to the Dardanelles, Africa, the Tigris, and other subsidiary theatres of war; and an important base was established at Dunkirk, whence countless air attacks were made on all military centres in Belgium. Many more R.N.A.S. squadrons, well provided with trained pilots and good machines, patrolled the East Coast while waiting for an opportunity of active service. This came early in 1917, when, under the wise supervision of the Air Board, the section of the Naval Air Service not concerned with naval matters was brought into close touch with the Royal Flying Corps, after it had pursued a lone trail for two years.

The Flying Corps units on the Western Front and elsewhere are now splendidly backed by help from the sister service. For the present purpose, therefore, the military efforts of the R.N.A.S. can be included with those of the R.F.C., after a tribute has been paid to the bombing offensives for which the Naval Air Service has always been famous, from early exploits with distant objectives such as Cuxhaven and Friedrichshafen to this year's successful attacks on German munition works, in conjunction with the French, and the countless trips from Dunkirk that are making the Zeebrugge-Ostend-Bruges sector such an unhappy home-from-home for U-boats, destroyers, and raiding aircraft.

Meanwhile the seaplane branch, about which little is heard, has reached a high level of efficiency. When the screen of secrecy is withdrawn from the North Sea, we shall hear very excellent stories of what the seaplanes have accomplished lately in the way of scouting, chasing the Zeppelin, and hunting the U-boat.

But from the nature of its purpose, the R.F.C. has borne the major part of our aerial burden during the war. In doing so, it has grown from a tiny band of enthusiasts and experimentalists to a great service which can challenge comparison with any other branch of the Army. The history of this attainment is intensely interesting.

The few dozen airmen who accompanied the contemptible little army on the retreat from Mons had no precedents from other campaigns to guide them, and the somewhat vague dictum that their function was to gather information had to be interpreted by pioneer methods. These were satisfactory under the then conditions of warfare, inasmuch as valuable information certainly was gathered during the retreat, when a blind move would have meant disaster,—how valuable only the chiefs of the hard-pressed force can say. This involved more than the average difficulties, for as the battle swayed back towards Paris new landing-grounds had to be sought, and temporary aerodromes improvised every few days.

The small collection of serviceable aeroplanes again justified themselves at the decisive stand in the Marne and Ourcq basin, where immediate reports of enemy concentrations were essential to victory. Again, after the Hun had been swept across the Aisne and was stretching north-eastward tentacles to clutch as much of the coast as was consonant with an unbroken line, the aerial spying out of the succeeding phases of retirement was of great service. Indeed, tentative though it was, the work of the British, French, and German machines before the advent of trench warfare proved how greatly air reconnaissance would alter the whole perspective of an open country campaign.

After the long barrier of trenches deadlocked the chances of extended movement and opened the dreary months of more or less stationary warfare, the R.F.C. organisation in France had time and space for self-development. Aerodromes were selected and erected, the older and less satisfactory types of machine were replaced by the stable B.E2.C., the active service squadrons were reconstructed and multiplied.

To the observation of what happened behind the actual front was added the mapping of the enemy's intricate trench-mosaic. For a month or two this was accomplished by the methodical sketches of a few observers. It was an exceedingly difficult task to trace every trench and sap and to pattern the network from a height of about 2000 feet, but the infantry found small ground for dissatisfaction as regards the accuracy or completeness of the observers' drawings. Then came the introduction of aerial photography on a large scale, and with it a complete bird's-eye plan of all enemy defence works, pieced together from a series of overhead snapshots that reproduced the complete trench-line, even to such details as barbed wire. By the infallible revelations of the camera, untricked by camouflage, concealed gun positions were spotted for the benefit of our artillery, and highly useful information about likely objectives was provided for the bombing craft.

The frequent bombing of German supply centres in Belgium and

North France came into being with the development of aerial photography. Owing to the difficulty of correct aim, before the advent of modern bomb-sights, all the early raids were carried out from a low altitude, sometimes from only a few hundred feet. For every purpose, moreover, low altitudes were the rule in the earlier months of the war, as most of the machines would not climb above 4000-7000 feet. Much of the observation was performed at something between 1000 and 2000 feet, so that aircraft often returned with a hundred or so bullet-holes in them.

Meanwhile the important work of artillery spotting was being developed. New systems of co-operation between artillery and aeroplanes were devised, tested, and improved. At first lamps or Very's lights were used to signal code-corrections, but these were soon replaced by wireless transmission from the observation machine. Targets which could not be ranged on through ground observation posts became targets no longer, after one shoot ranged from the air. As the number of available aircraft increased, so did the amount of observation for the guns, until finally the entire front opposite the British was registered for bombardment and divided into sections covered by specified artillery machines.

Aerial fighting, now so essential and scientific a branch of modern war, was rudimentary in 1914. Pilots and observers of the original Flying Corps carried revolvers, and many observers also equipped themselves with rifles, but the aeroplanes were not fitted with machine-guns. Such scraps as there were consisted of one machine manoeuvring round an opponent at close quarters for the chance of a well-aimed shot. Under these circumstances to "bring down" or "drive down out of control" an enemy was extremely difficult, though a very gallant officer, since killed in action, once killed two German pilots within five minutes with his revolver.

Soon the possibilities of aerial machine-guns were quickly recognised. The R.F.C. adopted the Lewis, which from the points of view of lightness and handiness was well suited for aircraft, and the German airmen countered with a modified Hotchkiss and other types.

But the stable observation machines, while excellent for reconnaissance and artillery spotting, allowed their crews only a small arc of fire, and not until the German single-seater scouts and our Bristol scout, then a comparatively fast machine, appeared on the western front in the spring of 1915 did the destruction of aeroplanes become an everyday occurrence. With the introduction of scouts for escort and protective duties came formation flying and concerted attack.

Fighting craft continued to increase in speed and numbers. As the struggle became more and more intense, so did the scene of it move higher and higher, prodded by an ever-growing capacity for climb and the ever-growing menace of the anti-aircraft guns. The average air battle of today begins at an altitude between 12,000 and 20,000 feet.

The conflict for mechanical superiority has had its ebb and flow, and consequently of its proportional casualties; but the British have never once been turned from their programme of observation. There have been critical times, as for example when the Fokker scourge of late 1915 and early 1916 laid low so many of the observation craft. But the Fokkers were satisfactorily dealt with by the de Haviland and the F.E.8. pusher scouts and the F.E. "battleplane," as the newspapers of the period delighted to call it. Next the pendulum swung towards the British, who kept the whip hand during the summer and autumn of last year. Even when the Boche again made a bid for ascendancy with the Halberstadt, the Roland, the improved L.V.G., and the modern Albatross scout, the Flying Corps organisation kept the situation well in hand, though the supply of faster machines was complicated by the claims of the R.N.A.S. squadrons in England.

Throughout the Somme Push we were able to maintain that aerial superiority without which a great offensive cannot succeed. This was partly the result of good organisation and partly of the fighting capabilities of the men who piloted the Sopwith, the Nieuport, the de Haviland, the F.E., and other 1916 planes which were continually at grips with the Hun. The German airmen, with their "travelling circuses" of twelve to fifteen fast scouts, once more had an innings in the spring of the current year, and the older types of British machine were hard put to it to carry through their regular work.

Then came the great day when scores of our new machines, husbanded for the occasion, engaged the enemy hell-for-leather at his own place in the air. An untiring offensive was continued by our patrols, and the temporary supremacy passed into British hands, where it very definitely remains, and where, if the shadows of coming events and the silhouettes of coming machines materialise, it is likely to remain.

Judged on a basis of losses, the unceasing struggle between aeroplane and aeroplane would seem to have been fairly equal, though it must be remembered that three-quarters of the fighting has had for its *milieu* the atmosphere above enemy territory. Judged on a basis of the maintenance of adequate observation, which is the primary object of aerial attack and defence, the British have won consistently. At no time has the R.F.C. been obliged to modify its duties of reconnaissance, artillery spotting, photography, or co-operation with advancing infantry, which was introduced successfully last summer. On the contrary, each of these functions, together with bombing and "ground stunts" from low altitudes, has swollen to an abnormal extent.

An idea of the vastness of our aerial effort on the British front in France can be gathered from the R.F.C. work performed on a typical "big push" day.

Throughout the night preceding an advance, several parties, laden with heavy bombs, steer by compass to Hun headquarters or other objectives, and return no longer laden with bombs. The first streak of daylight is the herald of an exodus from west to east of many score fighting craft. These cross the lines, hover among the Archie bursts, and drive back or down all black-crossed strangers within sight. Some of them go farther afield and attack the Boche above his own aerodromes. Such enemy craft as manage to take the air without meeting trouble from the advanced offensive patrols are tackled by the scouts near the lines. The few that travel still farther eastward with the intention of swooping on our observation machines, or of themselves gathering information, receive a hearty welcome from our defensive patrols.

The British two-seaters are thus free to direct the artillery, link the attacking infantry with headquarters, and spy out the land. As soon as the early morning light allows, a host of planes will be darting backward and forward over the trench-line as they guide the terrific bombardment preliminary to an attack. Other machines are searching for new emplacements and signs of preparation behind the enemy trenches. Several formations carry out tactical reconnaissances around an area stretching from the lines to a radius twenty miles east of them, and further parties perform strategic reconnaissance by covering the railways, roads, and canals that link the actual front with bases thirty to ninety miles behind it.

When, at a scheduled time, the infantry emerge over the top behind a curtain of shells, the contact patrol buses follow their doings, inform the gunners of any necessary modifications in the barrage, or of some troublesome nest of machine-guns, note the positions held by the attackers, collect signals from the battalion headquarters, and by means of message bags dropped over brigade headquarters report progress to the staff. If, later, a further advance be made, the low-flying contact machines again play their part of mothering the infantry.

Machines fitted with cameras photograph every inch of the defences improvised by the enemy, and, as insurance against being caught unprepared by a counter-attack, an immediate warning of whatever movement is in evidence on the lines of communication will be supplied by the reconnaissance observers. Under the direction of artillery squadrons the guns pound the new Boche front line and range on troublesome batteries.

The bombing craft are responsible for onslaughts on railways, supply *depôts*, garrison towns, headquarters, aerodromes, and chance targets. Other guerrilla work is done by craft which, from a height of anything under a thousand feet, machine-gun whatever worthwhile objects they spot. A column of troops on the march, transport, ammunition waggons, a train, a stray motor-car—all these are greeted joyfully by the pilots who specialise in ground stunts. And at every hour of daylight the scouts and fighting two-seaters protect the remainder of the R.F.C. by engaging all Huns who take to the air.

Doubtless, when sunset has brought the roving birds back to their nest, there will be a few "missing"; but this, part of the day's work, is a small enough sacrifice for the general achievement—the staff supplied with quick and accurate information, a hundred or two Boche batteries silenced, important works destroyed, enemy communications impeded, a dozen or so black-crossed aeroplanes brought down, valuable photographs and reports obtained, and the ground-Hun of every species harried.

The German Flying Corps cannot claim to perform anything like the same amount of aerial observation as its British counterpart. It is mainly occupied in fighting air battles and hampering the foreign machines that spy on their army. To say that the German machines are barred altogether from reconnaissance and artillery direction would be exaggeration, but not wild exaggeration. Seldom can an enemy plane call and correct artillery fire for longer than half an hour. From time to time a fast machine makes a reconnaissance tour at a great height, and from time to time others dart across the lines for photography, or to search for gun positions.

An appreciable proportion of these do not return. Four-fifths of the Hun bomb raids behind our front take place at night-time, when comparative freedom from attack is balanced by impossibility of accurate aim. Apart from these spasmodic activities, the German pilots concern themselves entirely with attempts to prevent allied observation. They have never yet succeeded, even during the periods of their nearest approach to the so-called "mastery of the air," and probably they never will succeed. The advantages attendant upon a maintenance of thorough observation, while whittling down the enemy's to a minimum, cannot be overestimated.

To determine how much credit for the brilliant achievement I have tried to outline belongs to the skill and adaptability of British airmen, and how much to successful organisation, would be difficult and rather unnecessary. But it is obvious that those who guided the R.F.C. from neglected beginnings to the status of a great air service had a tremendous task. Only the technical mind can realise all that it has involved in the production of trained personnel, aeroplanes, engines, aircraft *depôts*, aerodromes, wireless equipment, photographic workshops and accessories, bombs, and a thousand and one other necessaries.

Many thousand pilots have been trained in all the branches of war flying. The number of squadrons now in France would surprise the layman if one were allowed to make it public; while other squadrons have done excellent work in Macedonia, Egypt, Mesopotamia, East Africa, and elsewhere. Mention must also be made of the Home Defence groups, but for which wholesale Zeppelin raids on the country would be of common occurrence.

How to make best use of the vast personnel in France is the business of the staff, who link the fighting members of the corps with the Intelligence Department and the rest of the Army in the field. To them has fallen the introduction and development of the various functions of war aircraft, besides the planning of bomb raids and concerted aerial offensives. On the equipment side there is an enormous wastage to be dealt with, and consequently a constant cross-Channel interchange of machines. The amount of necessary replacement is made specially heavy by the short life of effective craft. A type of machine is good for a few months of active service, just holds its own for a few more, and then becomes obsolete except as a training bus. To surpass or even keep pace with the Boche Flying Corps on the mechanical side, it has been necessary for the supply department to do a brisk trade in new ideas and designs, experiment, improvement, and scrapping.

Although free-lance attacks by airmen on whatever takes their fancy down below are now common enough, they were unknown little over a year ago. Their early history is bound up with the introduction of contact patrols, or co-operation with advancing infantry. Previous to the Somme Push of 1916, communication during an attack between infantry on the one hand and the guns and various headquarters on the other was a difficult problem. A battalion would go over the top and disappear into the enemy lines. It might have urgent need of reinforcements or of a concentrated fire on some dangerous spot. Yet to make known its wants quickly was by no means easy, for the telephone wires were usually cut, carrier-pigeons went astray, and runners were liable to be shot. When the British introduced the "creeping barrage" of artillery pounding, which moved a little ahead of the infantry and curtained them from machine-gun and rifle fire, the need for rapid communication was greater than ever. Exultant attackers would rush forward in advance of the programmed speed and be mown by their own barrage.

Credit for the trial use of the aeroplane to link artillery with infantry belongs to the British, though the French at Verdun first brought the method to practical success. We then developed the idea on the Somme with notable results. Stable machines, equipped with wireless transmitters and Klaxon horns, flew at a low height over detailed sectors, observed all developments, signalled back guidance for the barrage, and by means of message bags supplied headquarters with valuable information. Besides its main purpose of mothering the infantry, the new system of contact patrols was found to be useful in dealing with enemy movements directly behind the front line. If the bud of a counter-attack appeared, aeroplanes would call upon the guns to nip it before it had time to blossom.

Last September we of the fighting and reconnaissance squadrons began to hear interesting yarns from the corps squadrons that specialised in contact patrols. An observer saved two battalions from extinction by calling up reinforcements in the nick of time. When two tanks slithered around the ruins of Courcelette two hours before the razed village was stormed, the men in the trenches would have known nothing of this unexpected advance-guard but for a contact machine. The pilot and observer of another bus saw two tanks converging eastward at either end of a troublesome Boche trench. A German officer, peering round a corner, drew back quickly when he found one of the new steel beasts advancing. He hurried to an observation post round a bend in the lines.

Arrived there, he got the shock of his life when he found a second metal monster waddling towards him. Alarmed and unnerved, he probably ordered a retirement, for the trench was evacuated immediately. The observer in a watching aeroplane then delivered a much-condensed synopsis of the comedy to battalion headquarters, and the trench was peacefully occupied.

Inevitably the nearness of the enemy to machines hovering over a given area bred in the airmen concerned a desire to swoop down and panic the Boche. Movement in a hostile trench was irresistible, and many a pilot shot off his engine, glided across the lines, and let his observer spray with bullets the home of the Hun. The introduction of such tactics was not planned beforehand and carried out to order. It was the outcome of a new set of circumstances and almost unconscious enterprise. More than any other aspect of war flying, it is, I believe, this imminence of the unusual that makes the average war pilot swear greatly by his job, while other soldiers temper their good work with grousing. His actions are influenced by the knowledge that somewhere, behind a ridge of clouds, in the nothingness of space, on the patchwork ground, the True Romance has hidden a new experience, which can only be found by the venturer with alert vision, a quick brain, and a fine instinct for opportunity.

The free-lance ground stunt, then, had its origin in the initiative of a few pilots who recognised a chance, took it, and thus opened yet another branch in the huge departmental store of aerial tactics. The exploits of these pioneers were sealed with the stamp of official approval, and airmen on contact patrol have since been encouraged to relieve boredom by joyous pounces on Brother Boche.

The star turn last year was performed by a British machine that captured a trench. The pilot guided it above the said trench for some hundred yards, while the observer emptied drum after drum of ammunition at the crouching Germans. A headlong scramble was followed by the appearance of an irregular line of white billowings. The enemy were waving handkerchiefs and strips of material in token of surrender! Whereupon our infantry were signalled to take possession, which they did. Don't shrug your shoulders, friend the reader, and say: "Quite a good story, but tall, very tall." The facts were related in the R.F.C. section of *Comic Cuts*, otherwise G.H.Q. summary of work.

Fighting squadrons soon caught the craze for ground stunts and carried it well beyond the lines. One machine chased a train for miles a few hundred feet above, derailed it, and spat bullets at the lame coaches until driven off by enemy craft. Another made what was evidently an inspection of troops by some Boche Olympian look like the riotous disorder of a Futurist painting. A pilot with some bombs to spare spiralled down over a train, dropped the first bomb on the engine, and the second, third, fourth, and fifth on the soldiers who scurried from the carriages. When a detachment of cavalry really did break through for once in a while, it was startled to find an aerial vanguard. A frolicsome biplane darted ahead, pointed out positions worthy of attack, and created a diversion with Lewis gun fire.

At the end of a three-hour offensive patrol my pilot would often descend our bus to less than a thousand feet, cross No Man's Land again, and zigzag over the enemy trenches, where we disposed of surplus ammunition to good purpose. On cloudy days, with the pretext of testing a new machine or a gun, he would fly just above the clouds, until we were east of the lines, then turn round and dive suddenly through the cloud-screen in the direction of the Boche positions, firing his front gun as we dropped. The turn of my rear gun came afterwards when the pilot flattened out and steered northward along the wrong border of No Man's Land. Once, when flying very low, we looked into a wide trench and saw a group of tiny figures make confused attempts to take cover, tumbling over each other the while in ludicrous confusion.

I remember a notable first trip across the lines made by a pilot who had just arrived from England. He had been sent up to have a look at the battle line, with an old-hand observer and instructions not to cross the trenches. However, he went too far east, and found himself ringed by Archie bursts. These did not have their customary effect on a novice of inspiring mortal funk, for the new pilot became furiously angry and flew Berserk. He dived towards Bapaume, dropped unscathed through the barrage of anti-aircraft shelling for which this stronghold was at the time notorious, fired a hundred rounds into the town square from a height of 800 feet, and raced back over the Bapaume-Pozières road pursued by flaming "onion" rockets. The observer recovered from his surprise in time to loose off a drum of ammunition at Bapaume, and three more along the straight road to the front line, paying special attention to the village of Le Sars.

It was above this village that I once was guilty of communicating with the enemy. During a three-hours' offensive patrol around the triangle—Bapaume-Mossy-Face Wood-Epehy—we had not seen a single Hun machine. Low clouds held Archie in check, and there was therefore small necessity to swerve from a straight course. Becoming bored, I looked at the pleasant-seeming countryside below, and reflected how ill its appearance harmonised with its merits as a dwelling-place, judged on the best possible evidence—the half-hysterical diaries found on enemy prisoners, the bitter outpourings anent the misery of intense bombardment and slaughter, the ominous title "The Grave" given to the region by Germans who had fought there. An echo of light-hearted incursions into German literature when I was a student at a Boche college suggested that the opening lines of Schiller's "Sehnsucht" were peculiarly apposite to the state of mind of the Huns who dwelt by the Somme.

Wishing to share my discovery, I wrote the verse in large block capitals, ready to be dropped at a convenient spot. I took the liberty of transposing three pronouns from the first person to the second, so as to apostrophise our Boche brethren. The patrol finished, my pilot spiralled down to within a 300-yard range of the ground and flew along the road past Martinpuich, while I pumped lead at anything that might be a communication trench. We sprinkled Le Sars with bullets, and there I threw overboard the quotation from a great German poet, folded inside an empty Very's cartridge to which I had attached canvas streamers. If it was picked up, I trust the following lines were not regarded merely as wordy frightfulness:

Ach! aus dieses Thales Gründen
Die der kalte Nebel drückt,
Könnt' ihr doch den Ausgang finden,
Ach! wie fühlt' ihr euch beglückt!

Of all the tabloid tales published last year in R.P.C. *Comic Cuts*, the most comic was that of a mist, a British bus, and a Boche General. The mist was troublesome; the bus, homeward bound after a reconnaissance, was flying low to keep a clear vision of the earth; the general was seated in his dignified car, after the manner of generals. The British pilot dived on the car, the British observer fired on the car, the Boche chauffeur stopped the car, the Boche general jumped from the car. Chauffeur and general rushed through a field into a wood; pilot and observer went home and laughed.

Thus far the facts are taken from the official report. An appropriate supplement was the rumour, which deserved to be true but possibly wasn't, that the observer turned in the direction of the vanished general and plagiarised George Robey with a shout into the unhearing air: "Cheeriho old thing, here's a go, my hat, priceless!"

So much for past accomplishment. The future of war flying, like all futures, is problematical; but having regard to our present unquestionable superiority in the air, and to the blend of sane imagination and practical ability now noticeable as an asset of the flying services directorate, one can hazard the statement that in the extended aerial war which is coming the R.F.C. and R.N.A.S. will nearly satisfy the most exacting of critics.

The tendency is toward a rapid development of aircraft even more startling than that of the past. Some of the modern scout machines have a level speed of 130-150 miles an hour, and can climb more than 1000 feet a minute until an abnormal height is reached. It is certain that within a year later machines will travel 160, 180, and 200 miles an hour level. Quantity as well as quality is on the up-grade, so that the power to strike hard and far will increase enormously, helped by heavier armament, highly destructive bombs, and more accurate bomb-sights.

And, above all, we shall see a great extension of ground attacks by air cavalry. The production of a machine specially adapted for this purpose, armoured underneath, perhaps, and carrying guns that fire downward through the fuselage, is worth the careful attention of aeroplane designers. It is probable that with the reappearance of extended military movement on the western front, as must happen sooner or later, continuous guerrilla tactics by hundreds of low-flying aeroplanes may well turn an orderly retirement into a disorderly rout.

When and if a push of pushes really breaks the German line, I fully expect that we of the air service will lead the armies of pursuit and make ourselves a pluperfect nuisance to the armies of retreat. Temporary second lieutenants may yet be given the chance to drive a Boche general or two into the woods, or even—who can limit the freaks of Providence?—plug down shots at the Limelight *Kaiser* himself, as he tours behind the front in his favourite *rôle* of *Bombastes Furioso*.

CHAPTER 8

The Daily Round

During a bout of active service one happens upon experiences that, though they make no immediate impression, become more prominent than the most dramatic events, when the period is past and can be viewed in retrospect. Sub-consciousness, wiser than the surface brain, penetrates to the inner sanctuary of true values, photographs something typical of war's many aspects, places the negative in the dark room of memory, and fades into inertia until again called upon to act as arbiter of significance for everyday instinct. Not till long later, when released from the tension of danger and abnormal endeavour, is one's mind free to develop the negative and produce a clear photograph. The sensitive freshness of the print then obtained is likely to last a lifetime. I leave a detailed explanation of this process to the comic people who claim acquaintance with the psychology of the immortal soul; for my part, I am content to remain a collector of such mental photographs.

A few examples of the subconscious impressions gathered during my last year's term at the Front are the curious smile of a dead observer as we lifted his body from a bullet-plugged machine; the shrieking of the wires whenever we dived on Hun aircraft; a tree trunk falling on a howitzer; a line of narrow-nosed buses, with heavy bombs fitted under the lower planes, ready to leave for their objective; the ghostliness of Ypres as we hovered seven thousand feet above its ruins; a certain riotous evening when eight of the party of fourteen ate their last dinner on earth; a severe reprimand delivered to me by a meticulous colonel, after I returned from a long reconnaissance that included four air flights, for the crime of not having fastened my collar before arrival on the aerodrome at 5 a.m.; a broken Boche aeroplane falling in two segments at a height of ten thousand feet; the breathless moments at a Base hospital when the surgeon-in-charge examined new casualties to decide which of them were to be sent across the Channel; and clearest of all, the brown-faced infantry marching back to the trenches from our village.

A muddy, unkempt battalion would arrive in search of rest and recuperation. It distributed itself among houses, cottages, and barns, while the Frenchwomen looked sweet or sour according to their diverse tempers, and whether they kept estaminets, sold farm produce, had husbands *là-bas*, or merely feared for their poultry and the cleanliness of their homes. Next day the exhausted men would reappear as *beaux sabreurs* with bright buttons, clean if discoloured tunics, and a jaunty, untired walk. The drum and fife band practised in the tiny square before an enthusiastic audience of *gamins*. Late every afternoon the aerodrome was certain to be crowded by inquisitive Tommies, whose peculiar joy it was to watch a homing party land and examine the machines for bullet marks. The officers made overtures on the subject of joy-rides, or discussed transfers to the Flying Corps. Interchange of mess courtesies took place, attended by a brisk business in yarns and a mutual appreciation of the work done by R.F.C. and infantry.

Then, one fine day, the drum and fife rhythm of "A Long, Long Trail" would draw us to the roadside, while our friends marched away to Mouquet Farm, or Beaumont Hamel, or Hohenzollern Redoubt, or some other point of the changing front that the Hun was about to lose. And as they left, the men were mostly silent; though they looked debonair enough with their swinging quickstep and easy carriage, and their frying-pan hats set at all sorts of rakish angles. Their officers would nod, glance enviously at the apple-trees and tents in our pleasant little orchard, and pass on to the front of the Front, and all that this implied in the way of mud, vermin, sudden death, suspense, and damnable discomfort. And returning to the orchard we offered selfish thanks to Providence in that we were not as the millions who hold and take trenches.

The flying officer in France has, indeed, matter for self-congratulation when compared with the infantry officer, as anyone who has served in both capacities will bear witness. Flying over enemy country is admittedly a strain, but each separate job only lasts from two to four hours. The infantryman in the front line is trailed by risk for the greater part of twenty-four hours daily. His work done, the airman returns to fixed quarters, good messing, a bath, plenty of leisure, and a real bed. The infantry officer lives mostly on army rations, and as often as not he sleeps in his muddy clothes, amid the noise of war, after a long shift crammed with uncongenial duties.

As regards actual fighting the airman again has the advantage. For those with a suitable temperament there is tense joy in an air scrap; there is none in trudging along a mile of narrow communication trench, and then, arrived at one's unlovely destination, being perpetually *ennuied* by crumps and other devilries. And in the game of poker played with life, death, and the will to destroy, the airman has but to reckon with two marked cards—the Ace of Clubs, representing Boche aircraft, and the Knave Archibald; whereas, when the infantryman stakes his existence, he must remember that each sleeve of the old cheat Death contains half a dozen cards.

All this by way of prelude to a protest against the exaggerative ecstasies indulged in by many civilians when discussing the air services. The British pilots are competent and daring, but they would be the last to claim an undue share of war's glory. Many of them deserve the highest praise; but then so do many in all other fighting branches of Army and Navy. An example of what I mean is the reference to R.F.C. officers, during a Parliamentary debate, as "*the super-heroes of the war,*"—a term which, for ungainly absurdity, would be hard to beat. To those who perpetrate such far-fetched phrases I would humbly say:

"Good gentlemen, we are proud to have won your approval, but for the Lord's sake don't make us ridiculous in the eyes of other soldiers."

Yet another asset of the airman is that his work provides plenty of scope for the individual, who in most sections of the Army is held on the leash of system and co-operation. The war pilot, though subject to the exigencies of formation flying, can attack and manoeuvre as he pleases. Most of the star performers are individualists who concentrate on whatever methods of destroying an enemy best suit them.

Albert Ball, probably the most brilliant air fighter of the war, was the individualist *in excelsis*. His deeds were the outcome partly of pluck—certainly not of luck—but mostly of thought, insight, experiment, and constant practice. His knowledge of how to use sun, wind, and clouds, coupled with an instinct for the "blind side" of whatever Hun machine he had in view, made him a master in the art of approaching unobserved. Arrived at close quarters, he usually took up his favourite position under the German's tail before opening fire. His experience then taught him to anticipate any move that an unprepared enemy might make, and his quick wits how to take advantage of it.

Last autumn, whenever the weather kept scout machines from their patrols but was not too bad for joy-flying, he would fly near the aerodrome and practise his pet manoeuvres for hours at a time. In the early days of Ball's dazzling exploits his patrol leader once complained, after an uneventful trip, that he left the formation immediately it crossed the lines, and stayed away until the return journey. Ball's explanation was that throughout the show he remained less than two hundred feet below the leader's machine, "practising concealment."

The outstanding pilots of my old squadron were all individualists in attack, and it was one of my hobbies to contrast their tactics. C., with his blind fatalism and utter disregard of risk, would dive a machine among any number of Huns, so that he usually opened a fight with an advantage of startling audacity. S., another very successful leader, worked more in co-operation with the machines behind him, and took care to give his observer every chance for effective fire. His close watch on the remainder of the formation saved many a machine in difficulties from disaster. V., my pilot and flight-commander, was given to a quick dive at the enemy, a swerve aside, *a recul pour mieux sauter*, a vertical turn or two, and another dash to close grips from an unexpected direction, while I guarded the tail-end.

But writing reminiscences of *Umpty* Squadron's early days is a melancholy business. When it was first formed all the pilots were picked men, for the machines were the best British two-seaters then in existence, and their work throughout the autumn push was to be more dangerous than that of any squadron along the British front. The price we paid was that nine weeks from our arrival on the Somme only nine of the original thirty-six pilots and observers remained. Twelve officers flew to France with the flight to which I belonged. Six weeks after their first job over the lines I was one of the only two survivors. Three of the twenty-five who dropped out returned to England with wounds or other disabilities; the rest, closely followed by twenty of those who replaced them, went to Valhalla, which is half-way to heaven; or to Karlsruhe, which is between hell and Freiburg-im-Brisgau.

And the reward? One day, in a letter written by a captured Boche airman, was found the sentence: "The most-to-be-feared of British machines is the S——." The umptieth squadron then had the only machines of this type in France.

During the short period of their stay with us, the crowd of boys thus rudely snatched away were the gayest company imaginable; and, indeed, they were boys in everything but achievement. As a patriarch of twenty-four I had two more years to my discredit than the next oldest among the twelve members of our flight-mess. The youngest was seventeen and a half. Our Squadron Commander, one of the finest men I have met in or out of the army, became a lieutenant-colonel at twenty-five. Even he was not spared, being killed in a flying accident some months later.

Though we were all such good friends, the high percentage of machines "missing" from our hangars made us take the abnormal casualties almost as a matter of course at the time. One said a few words in praise of the latest to go, and passed on to the next job. Not till the survivors returned home did they have time, away from the stress of war, to feel keen sorrow for the brave and jolly company. For some strange reason, my own hurt at the loss was toned down by a mental farewell to each of the fallen, in words borrowed from the song sung by an old-time maker of ballads when youth left him: "*Adieu, la très gente compagne.*"

The crowded months of the *umptieth* squadron from June to November were worthwhile for the pilots who survived. The only two of our then flight-commanders still on the active list are now commanding squadrons, while all the subaltern pilots have become flight-commanders. The observers, members of a tribe akin to Kipling's Sergeant Whatsisname, are as they were in the matter of rank, needless to say.

For my part, on reaching Blighty by the grace of God and an injured knee, I decided that if my unworthy neck were doomed to be broken, I would rather break it myself than let someone else have the responsibility. It is as a pilot, therefore, that I am about to serve another sentence overseas. A renewal of Archie's acquaintance is hardly an inviting prospect, but with a vivid recollection of great days with the old umptieth squadron, I shall not be altogether sorry to leave the hierarchy of home instructordom for the good-fellowship of active service. In a few months' time, after a further period of aerial outings, I hope to fill some more pages of *Blackwood*,[1] subject always to the sanction of their editor, the *bon Dieu*, and the *mauvais diable* who will act as censor. Meanwhile, I will try to sketch the daily round of the squadron in which I am proud to have been an observer.

★ ★ ★ ★ ★ ★ ★ ★ ★

"Quarter to five, sir, and a fine morning. You're wanted on the

---

1. This narrative first appeared in *Blackwood's Magazine*.

aerodrome at a quarter past."

I sit up. A shiver, and a return beneath the blankets for five minutes' rumination. Dressing will be dashed unpleasant in the cold of dawn. The canvas is wet with the night's rain. The reconnaissance is a long one, and will take fully three hours. The air at 10,000 feet will bite hard. Must send a field postcard before we start. Not too much time, so out and on with your clothes. Life is rotten.

While dressing we analyse the weather, that pivot of our day-today existence. On the weather depends our work and leisure, our comparative risks and comparative safety. Last thing at night, first thing in the morning, and throughout the day we search the sky for a sign. And I cannot deny that on occasions a sea of low clouds, making impossible the next job, is a pleasant sight.

The pale rose of sunrise is smudging over the last flickerings of the grey night. Only a few wisps of cloud are about, and they are too high to bother us. The wind is slight and from the east, for which many thanks, as it will make easier the return half of the circuit.

We wrap ourselves in flying kit and cross the road to the aerodrome. There the band of leather-coated officers shiver while discussing their respective places in the formation. A bus lands and taxies to a shed. From it descends the Squadron Commander, who, with gumboots and a warm coat over his pyjamas, has been "trying the air." "Get into your machines," he calls. As we obey he enters his hut-office and phones the wing headquarters.

The major reappears, and the command "Start up!" is passed along the line of machines. Ten minutes later we head for the trenches, climbing as we travel.

It was cold on the ground. It was bitter at 5000 feet. It is damnable at 10,000 feet. I lean over the side to look at Arras, but draw back quickly as the frozen hand of the atmosphere slaps my face. My gloved hands grow numb, then ache profoundly when the warm blood brings back their power to feel. I test my gun, and the trigger-pressure is painful. Life is worse than rotten, it is beastly.

But the cold soon does its worst, and a healthy circulation expels the numbness from my fingers. Besides, once we are beyond the lines, the work on hand allows small opportunity to waste time on physical sensations. On this trip there is little interruption, thank goodness. Archie falls short of his average shooting, and we are able to outpace a group of some twelve Hun two-seaters that try to intercept us. The movement below is noted, the round is completed according to programme, and we turn westward and homeward.

Have you ever sucked bull's-eyes, respected sir or *madame*? If not, take it from me that the best time to try them is towards the end of a three-hour flight over enemy country. Five bull's-eyes are then far more enjoyable than a five-course meal at the Grand Babylon Hotel. One of these striped vulgarities both soothes and warms me as we re-cross the trenches.

Down go the noses of our craft, and we lose height as the leader, with an uneven, tree-bordered road as guide, makes for Doulens. From this town our aerodrome shows up plainly towards the south-west. Soon we shall be in the mess marquee, behind us a completed job, before us a hot breakfast. Life is good.

Arrived on land we are met by mechanics, each of whom asks anxiously if his particular bus or engine has behaved well. The observers write their reports, which I take to the Brass Hats at headquarters. This done, I enter the orchard, splash about in a canvas bath, and so to a contented breakfast.

Next you will find most of the squadron officers at the aerodrome, seated in deck-chairs and warmed by an early autumn sun. It is the most important moment of the day—the post has just arrived. All letters except the one from His Majesty's impatient Surveyor of Taxes, who threatens to take proceedings "in the district in which you reside," are read and re-read, from "My dearest Bill" to "Yours as ever." Every scrap of news from home has tremendous value. Winkle, the dinky Persian with a penchant for night life, has presented the family with five kittens. Splendid! Lady X., who is, you know, the bosom friend of a certain Minister's wife, says the war will be over by next summer at the *latest*. Splendid again! Life is better than good, it is amusing.

Yesterday's London papers have been delivered with the letters. These also are devoured, from light leaders on electoral reform to the serious legends underneath photographs of the Lady Helen Toutechose, Mrs. Alexander Innit, and Miss Margot Rheingold as part-time nurses, canteeners, munitioners, flag-sellers, charity matinee programme sellers, *tableaux vivants*, and patronesses of the undying arts. Before turning to the latest number of the *Aeroplane*, our own particular weekly, one wonders idly how the Lady Helen Toutechose and her emulators, amid their strenuous quick-change war-work, find time to be photographed so constantly, assiduously, and distractingly.

We pocket our correspondence and tackle the morning's work. Each pilot makes sure that his machine is overhauled, and if necessary, he runs the engine or puts a re-rigged bus through its paces. I am told off to instruct half a dozen officers newly arrived from the trenches on how to become a reliable reconnaissance observer in one week. Several of us perform mysteriously in the workshops, for we are a squadron of many inventors.

Every other officer has a pet mechanical originality. Marmaduke is preparing a small gravity tank for his machine, to be used when the pressure tank is ventilated by a bullet. The Tripehound has a scheme whereby all the control wires can be duplicated. Someone else has produced the latest thing in connections between the pilot's joystick and the Vickers gun. I am making a spade-grip trigger for the Lewis gun, so that the observer can always have one hand free to manipulate the movable back-sight. When one of these deathless inventions is completed the real hard work begins. The new gadget is adopted unanimously by the inventor himself, but he has a tremendous task in making the rest of the squadron see its merits.

After lunch we scribble letters, for the post leaves at five. As we write the peaceful afternoon is disturbed by the roar of five engines. B Flight is starting up in readiness for an offensive patrol. Ten minutes later more engines break into song, as three machines of C Flight leave to photograph some new lines of defence before Bapaume. The overhead hum dies away, and I allow myself a sleep in payment of the early morning reconnaissance.

Wearing a dress suit I am seated on the steps of a church. On my knee is a Lewis gun. An old gentleman, very respectable in dark spats, a black tie, and shiny top-hat, looks down at me reproachfully.

"Very sad," he murmurs.

"Don't you think this trigger's a damned good idea?" I ask.

"Young man, this is an outrage. As you are not ashamed enough to leave the churchyard of your own accord, I shall have you turned out."

I laugh and proceed to pass some wire through the pistol-grip. The old man disappears, but he returns with three grave-diggers, who brandish their spades in terrifying manner. "Ha!" I think, "I must fly away." I fly my wings (did I tell you I had wings?) and rise above the church tower. Archie has evidently opened fire, for I hear a near-by *wouff*. I try to dodge, but it is too late. A shell fragment strikes my nose. Much to my surprise I find I can open my eyes. My nose is sore, one side of the tent waves gently, and a small apple reposes on my chest.

Having run into the open I discover that the disengaged members of C Flight are raiding our corner with the sour little apples of the orchard. We collect ammunition from a tree and drive off the attackers. A diversion is created by the return of the three photography machines. We troop across to meet them.

The next scene is the aerodrome once again. We sit in a group and censor letters. The countryside is quiet, the sun radiates cheerfulness, and the war seems very remote. But the mechanics of B Flight stand outside their sheds and look east. It is time the offensive patrol party were back.

"There they are," says a watcher. Three far-away specks grow larger and larger. As they draw near, we are able to recognise them as our buses, by the position of their struts and the distinctive drone of their engines.

Four machines crossed the lines on the expedition; where is the fourth? The crew of the other three do not know. They last saw the missing craft ten miles behind the Boche trenches, where it turned west after sending up a Very's light to signal the necessity of an immediate return. There were no Huns in sight, so the cause must have been engine trouble.

The shadows of the lost pilot and observer darken the first ten minutes at the dinner-table. However, since cheerfulness is beyond godliness, we will take this to be an anxious occasion with a happy ending. Comes a welcome message from the orderly officer, saying that the pilot has phoned. His reason for leaving the patrol was that his engine went dud. Later it petered out altogether, so that he was forced to glide down and land near a battery of our howitzers.

The conversational atmosphere now lightens. Some people from another squadron are our guests, and with them we exchange the latest flying gossip. The other day, X rammed a machine after his gun had jammed. Y has been given the Military Cross. Archie has sent west two machines of the eleventh squadron. While on his way home, with no more ammunition, Z was attacked by a fast scout. He grabbed a Very's pistol and fired at the Boche a succession of lights, red, white, and green. The Boche, taking the rockets for a signal from a decoy machine, or from some new form of British frightfulness, promptly retired.

Dinner over, the usual crowd settle around the card-table, and the gramophone churns out the same old tunes. There is some dissension between a man who likes music and another who prefers rag-time. Number one leads off with the Peer Gynt Suite, and number two counters with the record that choruses: "Hello, how are you?" From the babble of yarning emerges the voice of our licensed liar—

"So I told the General he was the sort of bloke who ate tripe and gargled with his beer."

"Flush," calls a poker player.

"Give us a kiss, give us a kiss, by wireless," pleads the gramophone.

"Goodnight, chaps. See you over Cambrai." This from a departing guest.

Chorus—"Goodnight, old bean."

A somewhat wild evening ends with a sing-song, of which the star number is a ballad to the tune of "Tarpaulin Jacket," handed down from the pre-war days of the Flying Corps, and beginning—

The young aviator was dying,
And as 'neath the wreckage he lay (he lay),
To the A.M.'s assembled around him
These last parting words he did say:
'Take the cylinders out of my kidneys,
The connecting-rod out of my brain (my brain),
From the small of my back take the crank-shaft.
And assemble the engine again.'

On turning in we give the sky a final scour. It is non-committal on the subject of tomorrow's weather. The night is dark, the moon is at her last quarter, only a few stars glimmer.

I feel sure the land needs rain. If it be fine tomorrow we shall sit over Archie for three hours. If it be conveniently wet we shall charter a light tender and pay a long-deferred visit to the city of Arrière. There I shall visit a real barber; pass the time of day with my friend Henriette, whose black eyes and ready tongue grace a book shop of the Rue des Trois Cailloux; dine greatly at a little restaurant in the Rue du Corps Nu Sans Tête; and return with reinforcements of Anatole France, collar-studs, and French slang.

Letters From the Somme

Acknowledgment Is Due
To the
Owner of These Letters, Who Has Allowed
Me to Revise for Publication What
Was Written for Her Alone

1.

LOOKING FOR TROUBLE

. . . You have asked me, *mon amie*, to tell you, from personal experience, all about aeroplanes on active service. With the best will in the world I can do no such thing, any more than a medical student could tell you, from personal experience, all about midwifery.

The Flying Corps has in France hundreds of aeroplanes, scores of squadrons, and a dozen varying duties. Earlier in the war, when army aircraft were few and their function belonged to the pioneer stage, every pilot and observer dabbled in many things—reconnaissance, artillery observation, bomb raids, photography, and fighting. But the service has since expanded so much, both in size and importance, that each squadron is made to specialise in one or two branches of work, while other specialists look after the remainder. The daily round of an artillery squadron, for example, is very different from the daily round of a reconnaissance squadron, which is quite as different from that of a scout squadron. *Alors*, my experience only covers the duties of my own squadron. These I will do my best to picture for you, but please don't look upon my letters as dealing with the Flying Corps as a whole.

Perhaps you will see better what I mean if you know something

173

of our organisation and of the different kinds of machines. There are slow, stable two-seaters that observe around the lines; fighting two-seaters that operate over an area extending some thirty miles beyond the lines; faster fighting two-seaters that spy upon enemy country still farther afield; the bombing craft, single-seaters or two-seaters used as single-seaters; photography machines; and single-seater scouts, quick-climbing and quick-manoeuvring, that protect and escort the observation buses and pounce on enemy aeroplanes at sight. All these confine themselves to their specialised jobs, though their outgoings are planned to fit the general scheme of aerial tactics. The one diversion shared by every type is scrapping the air Hun whenever possible—and the ground Hun too for that matter, if he appear in the open and one can dive at him.

Our organisation is much the same as the organisation of the older—and junior—arms of the Service (oh yes! the Gazette gives us precedence over the Guards, the Household Cavalry, and suchlike people). Three or more squadrons are directed by a wing-commander, whom one treats with deep respect as he speeds a formation from the aerodrome; a number of wings, with an aircraft *depôt*, are directed by a brigadier, whom one treats with still deeper respect when he pays a visit of inspection; the whole is directed by the General-Officer-Commanding-the-Flying-Corps-in-the-Field, one-of-the-best, who treats us like brothers.

We, in *Umpty* squadron, are of the G.H.Q. wing, our work being long reconnaissance and offensive patrols over that part of the Somme basin where bands of Hun aircraft rove thickest. Our home is a wide aerodrome, flanked by a village that comprises about thirty decrepit cottages and a beautiful little old church. Our tents are pitched in a pleasant orchard, which is strewn with sour apples and field kitchens. For the rest, we are a happy family, and the sole blot on our Arcadian existence is the daily journey east to meet Brother Boche and his hired bully Archibald.

After which explanatory stuff I will proceed to what will interest you more,—the excitements and tediousness of flights over enemy country. Three hours ago I returned from a patrol round Mossy-Face Wood, where one seldom fails to meet black-crossed birds of prey, so I will begin with the subject of a hunt for the Flying Deutschman.

There are two kinds of fighting air patrol, the defensive and the offensive, the pleasantly exciting and the excitingly unpleasant. The two species of patrol have of late kept the great majority of German craft away from our lines.

Airmen who look for trouble over enemy country seldom fail to find it, for nothing enrages the Boche more than the overhead drone of allied aircraft. Here, then, are some average happenings on an offensive patrol, as I have known them.

We cross the lines at our maximum height, for it is of great advantage to be above an enemy when attacking. Our high altitude is also useful in that it makes us a small target for Herr Archie, which is distinctly important, as we are going to sit over him for the next few hours.

Archie only takes a few seconds to make up his mind about our height and range. He is not far wrong either, as witness the ugly black bursts slightly ahead, creeping nearer and nearer. Now there are two bursts uncomfortably close to the leader's machine, and its pilot and observer hear that ominous *wouff!* The pilot dips and swerves. Another *wouff!* and he is watching a burst that might have got him, had he kept a straight course.

Again the Archies try for the leader. This time their shells are well away, in fact so far back that they are near our bus. The German battery notices this, and we are forthwith bracketed in front and behind. We swoop away in a second, and escape with nothing worse than a violent stagger, and we are thrown upward as a shell bursts close underneath.

But we soon shake off the Archie group immediately behind the lines. Freed from the immediate necessity of shell-dodging, the flight-commander leads his covey around the particular hostile preserve marked out for his attention. Each pilot and each observer twists his neck as if it were made of rubber, looking above, below, and all around. Only thus can one guard against surprise and yet surprise strangers, and avoid being surprised oneself. An airman new to active service often finds difficulty in acquiring the necessary intuitive vision which attracts his eyes instinctively to hostile craft. If his machine straggles, and he has not this sixth sense, he will sometimes hear the rattle of a mysterious machine-gun, or even the phut of a bullet, before he sees the swift scout that has swooped down from nowhere.

There is a moment of excitement when the flight-commander spots three machines two thousand feet below. Are they Huns? His observer uses field-glasses, and sees black crosses on the wings. The signal to attack is fired, and we follow the leader into a steep dive.

With nerves taut and every faculty concentrated on getting near enough to shoot, and then shooting quickly but calmly, we have no time to analyse the sensations of that dive. We may feel the tremendous pressure hemming us in when we try to lean over the side, but otherwise all we realise is that the wind is whistling past the strained wires, that our guns must be ready for instant use, and that down below are some enemies.

The flight-commander, his machine aimed dead at the leading German, follows the enemy trio down, down, as they apparently seek to escape by going ever lower. He is almost near enough for some shooting, when the Huns dive steeply, with the evident intention of landing on a near-by aerodrome. One of them fires a light as he goes, and—enter the villain Archibald to loud music. A ter-rap!

Our old friend Archie has been lying in wait with guns set for a certain height, to which his three decoy birds have led us. There crashes a discord of shell-bursts as we pull our machines out of the dive and swerve away. The last machine to leave the unhealthy patch of air is pursued for some seconds by flaming rockets.

The patrol re-forms, and we climb to our original height. One machine has left for home, with part of a control wire dangling helplessly beneath it, and a chunk of tail-plane left as a tribute to Archie.

We complete the course and go over it again, with nothing more exciting than further anti-aircraft fire, a few Huns too low for another dive, and a sick observer.

Even intrepid birdmen (war correspondentese for flying officers) tire of trying to be offensive on a patrol, and by now we are varying our rubber-neck searchings with furtive glances at the time, in the hopes that the watch-hands may be in the home-to-roost position. At length the leader heads for the lines, and the lords of the air (more war correspondentese) forget their high estate and think of tea.

Not yet. Coming south towards Bapaume is a beautiful flock of black-crossed birds. As often happens, the German biplanes are ranged one above the other, like the tiers of a dress-circle.

Again the signal to attack, and the flight-commander sweeps at what seems to be the highest enemy. We are ranging ourselves round him, when two enemy scouts sweep down from heaven-knows-where, firing as they come. Several of their bullets enter the engine of our rearmost rearguard. Finding that the engine is on strike, the pilot detaches his machine from the confusion and glides across the lines, which are quite close.

For five minutes there is a medley of swift darts, dives, and cart-wheel turns, amid the continuous *ta-ta-ta-ta-ta* of machine-guns. Then a German machine sways, staggers, noses downward vertically, and rushes earthward, spinning rhythmically. The other Boches put their noses down and turn east. We follow until we find it impossible to catch them up, whereupon we make for home.

The trenches are now passed, and our aerodrome is quite near. The strained nerve-tension snaps, the air seems intoxicatingly light. Pilots and observers munch chocolate contentedly or lift up their voices in songs of Blighty. I tackle "The Right Side of Bond Street," and think of pleasant places and beings, such as Henley during regatta week, the Babylon Theatre, and your delightful self.

We land, piece together our report, and count the bullet-holes on the machine. In ten minutes' time you will find us around the mess-table, reconstructing the fight over late afternoon tea. In the intervals of eating cake I shall write you, and the gramo-phone will be shrilling "Chalk Farm to Camberwell Green."

France, July, 1916

2.

"ONE OF OUR MACHINES IS MISSING."

—*Official Report.*

. . . Much may be read into the ambiguous word "missing." Applied to a wife or an actress's jewellery it can mean any-thing. Applied to a man on active service it can mean one of three things. He may be dead, he may be a prisoner, he may be wounded and a prisoner. If he be dead he enters Valhalla. If he be a prisoner and a wise man he enters a small cheque for the German Red Cross, as being the quickest way of letting his bankers and relations know he is alive.

A missing aeroplane no longer exists, in nine cases out of ten. Either it is lying in pieces on enemy ground, smashed by an uncontrolled fall, or it was burned by its former tenants when they landed, after finding it impossible to reach safety. Quite recently my pilot and I nearly had to do this, but were just able to glide across a small salient. I am thus qualified to describe a typical series of incidents preceding the announcement, "one of our machines is missing," and I do so in the hope that this may interest you, madam, as you flit from town to country, country to town, and so to bed.

A group of British machines are carrying out a long reconnaissance. So far nothing has happened to divert the observers from their notes and sketches, and a pilot congratulates himself that he is on a joy-ride. Next instant his sixth sense tells him there is something in the air quite foreign to a joy-ride. And there is. A thousand yards ahead some eight to twelve machines have appeared. The reconnaissance birds keep to their course, but all eyes are strained towards the newcomers. Within ten seconds it is established that they are foes. The observers put aside note-books and pencils, and finger their machine-guns expectantly.

On come the Germans to dispute the right of way. On go the British, not seeking a fight, but fully prepared to force a way through. Their job is to complete the reconnaissance, and not to indulge in superfluous air duels, but it will take a very great deal to turn them from their path.

Now the aggressors are within 300 yards, and firing opens. When the fight gets to uncomfortably close quarters the Boches move aside and follow the reconnaissance party, waiting for an opportunity to surround stragglers. Finally, some lucky shots by a British observer cause one of them to land in a damaged condition, whereupon the rest retire. The British machines finish their job and return with useful information.

But the party is no longer complete. The pilot who thought of joy-rides was in the rear machine, and the rear machine has disappeared. Two Huns cut him off when the rest began to follow the British formation.

His observer takes careful aim at the nearest enemy, and rattles through a whole drum as the German sweeps down and past, until he is out of range. The pilot vertical-turns the machine, and makes for the second Boche. But this gentleman, refusing to continue the fight alone, dives to join his companion. The pair of them hover about for a few minutes, and then disappear eastward.

The lonely pilot and observer look round and take their bearings.

"Where are the others?" shouts the pilot down the speaking-tube.

"Right away to the north; we are alone in the wicked world." Thus the observer's reply, handed across on a slip of paper.

Hoping to catch sight of the reconnaissance party, my friend the pilot opens his engine full out and begins to follow the course that remained to be covered. For ten minutes he continues the attempt to catch up, but as the only aeroplanes to be seen are coming up from an enemy aerodrome he decides to get back alone as quickly as possible. He turns due west.

The homing bird must fly in the teeth of a strong west wind. It struggles along gamely, and the pilot calculates that he may reach the lines within twenty-five minutes. But he has a queer feeling that trouble is ahead, and, like his observer, he turns his head around the horizon, so as not to be caught unprepared.

All goes well for five minutes, except for some nasty Archie shells. Then the two men see a flock of aircraft at a great height, coming from the north. Although black crosses cannot be spotted at this range, the shape and peculiar whiteness of the wings make it probable that the strangers are hostile. Possibly they are the very people who attacked and followed the reconnaissance formation.

Our pilot puts down the nose of his machine, and races westward. The strangers, making good use of their extra height, turn south-west and try to head him off. They gain quickly, and pilot and observer brace themselves for a fight against odds.

The Germans are now about 700 feet higher than my friends, and directly above them. Four enemies dive, at an average speed of 150 miles an hour, and from all directions the Britishers hear the rattle of machine-guns. The observer engages one of the Huns, and evidently gets in some good shooting, for it swerves away and lets another take its place. Meanwhile enemy bullets have crashed through two spars, shot away a rudder-control, and ripped several parts of the fuselage.

The black-crossed hawks cluster all around. There are two on the left, one on the right, one underneath the tail, and two above. A seventh Hun sweeps past in front, about eighty yards ahead. The pilot's gun rakes it from stem to stern as it crosses, and he gives a great shout as its petrol-tank begins to blaze and the enemy craft flings itself down, with a stream of smoke and another flame shooting out behind.

But his own petrol-tank has been plugged from the side, and his observer has a bullet in the left arm. The petrol supply is regulated by pressure, and, the pressure having gone when German bullets opened the tank, the engine gets less and less petrol, and finally ceases work.

To glide fifteen miles to the lines is clearly impossible. There is nothing for it but to accept the inevitable and choose a good landing-ground. The pilot pushes the joystick slowly forward and prepares to land.

The Germans follow their prey down, ready to destroy if by any chance its engine comes back to life, and it stops losing height. The observer tears up papers and maps, performs certain other duties whereby the enemy is cheated of booty, and stuffs all personal possessions into his pocket.

A medley of thoughts race across the observer's mind as the pilot S-turns the machine over the field he has chosen. A prisoner!—damnable luck—all papers destroyed—arm hurting—useless till end of war—how long will it last?—chances of escape—relieve parents' suspense—must write—due for leave—Marjorie—Piccadilly in the sunshine—rotten luck—was to be—make best of it—*Kismet!*

One duty remains. The observer digs into the petrol tank as they touch earth, and then runs round the machine. In a second the petrol is ablaze and the fuselage and wings are burning merrily. Germans rush up and make vain attempts to put out the fire. Soon nothing remains but charred debris, a discoloured engine, bits of metal and twisted wires.

My friends are seized, searched, and disarmed. They then shake hands with the German pilots, now heatedly discussing who was chiefly responsible for their success. The captive couple are lunched by the enemy airmen, who see that the wounded observer receives proper attention. At the risk of incensing some of your eat-'em-alive civilian friends, I may say we have plenty of evidence that the German Flying Corps includes many gentlemen.

Later my friends are questioned, searched again from head to toe, and packed off to Germany. Just now they are affected with deadly heart-sickness, due to the wearisome inaction of confinement in a hostile land, while we, their friends and brothers, continue to play our tiny parts in Armageddon.

I enclose their names, and that of the prison camp where they are lodged. Perhaps you will find time to send them some of your fast-dwindling luxuries, as you flit from town to country, country to town, and so to bed.

France, July, 1916

3.

A BOMB RAID

. . . What are your feelings, dear lady, as you watch the airships that pass in the night and hear the explosion of their bombs? At such a time the sensations of most people, I imagine, are a mixture of deep interest, deep anger, excitement, nervousness, and desire for revenge. Certainly they do not include speculation about the men who man the raiders.

And for their part, the men who man the raiders certainly do not speculate about you and your state of mind. When back home, some of them may wonder what feelings they have inspired in the people below, but at the time the job's the thing and nothing else matters.

Out here we bomb only places of military value, and do it mostly in the daytime, but I should think our experiences must have much in common with those of Zeppelin crews. I can assure you they are far more strenuous than yours on the ground.

Our bombing machines in France visit all sorts of places— forts, garrison towns, railway junctions and railheads, bivouac grounds, staff headquarters, factories, ammunition *depôts*, aerodromes, Zeppelin sheds, and naval harbours. Some objectives are just behind the lines, some are 100 miles away. There are also free-lance exploits, as when a pilot with some eggs to spare dives down to a low altitude and drops them on a train or a column of troops.

A daylight bomb raid is seldom a complete failure, but the results are sometimes hard to record. If an ammunition store blows up, or a railway station bursts into flames, or a train is swept off the rails and the lines cut, an airman can see enough to know he has succeeded. But if the bombs fall on something that does not explode or catch fire, it is almost impossible to note exactly what has been hit. Even a fire is hard to locate while one is running away from Archie and perhaps a few flaming onions.

Fighting machines often accompany the bombing parties as escort. The fighters guard the bombers until the eggs are dropped, and seize any chances of a scrap on the way back. It is only thus that I have played a part in raids, for our squadron does not add bombs to its other troubles. I will now tell you, my very dear friend, about one such trip.

The morning is clear and filled with sunshine, but a strong westerly wind is blowing. This will increase our speed on the outward journey, and so help to make the attack a surprise. Those low-lying banks of thick white clouds are also favourable to the factor of surprise.

It is just before midday, and we are gathered in a group near the machines, listening to the flight-commander's final directions. Punctually at noon the bombers leave the ground, climb to the rendezvous height, and arrange themselves in formation. The scout machines constituting the escort proper follow, and rise to a few hundred feet above the bombers. The whole party circles round the aerodrome until the signal strips for "Carry on" are laid out on the ground, when it heads for the lines.

At this point we, the fighting two-seaters, start up and climb to our allotted height. We are to follow the bombing party and act as a rearguard until the eggs have fallen. Afterwards, when the others have finished their little bit and get home to their tea, it will be our pleasant task to hang about between the lines and the scene of the raid, and deal with such infuriated Boche pilots as may take the air with some idea of revenge.

We travel eastwards, keeping well in sight of the bombers. The ridges of clouds become more numerous, and only through gaps can we see the trenches and other landmarks. Archie, also, can only see through the gaps, and, disconcerted by the low clouds, his performance is not so good as usual. But for a few shells, very wide of the mark, we are not interrupted, for there are no German craft in sight.

With the powerful wind behind us we are soon over the objective, a large wood some few miles behind the lines. The wood is reported to be a favourite bivouac ground, and it is surrounded by Boche aerodromes.

Now the bombers drop below the clouds to a height convenient for their job. As the wood covers an area of several square miles and almost any part of it may contain troops, there is no need to descend far before taking aim. Each pilot chooses a spot for his particular attention, for preference somewhere near the road that bisects the wood. He aligns his sights on the target, releases the bombs, and watches for signs of an interrupted lunch below.

It is quite impossible to tell the extent of the damage, for the raid is directed not against some definite object, but against an area containing troops, guns, and stores. The damage will be as much moral as material since nothing unnerves war-weary men more than to realise that they are never safe from aircraft. The guns get busy at once, for the wood contains a nest of Archies. Ugly black bursts surround the bombers, who swerve and zigzag as they run. When well away from the wood they climb back to us through the clouds.

We turn west and battle our way against the wind, now our foe. Half-way to the lines we wave an envious goodbye to the bombers and scouts, and begin our solitary patrol above the clouds.

We cruise all round the compass, hunting for Huns. Twice we see enemy machines through rifts in the clouds, but each time we dive towards them they refuse battle and remain at a height of some thousand feet, ready to drop even lower, if they can lure us down through the barrage of A.-A. shells. Nothing else of importance happens, and things get monotonous. I look at my watch and think it the slowest thing on earth, slower than the leave train. The minute-hand creeps round, and homing-time arrives.

We have one more flutter on the way to the trenches. Two Huns come to sniff at us, and we dive below the clouds once more.

But it is the old, old dodge of trying to salt the bird's tail. The Hun decoys make themselves scarce—and H.E. bursts make themselves plentiful. Archie has got the range of those clouds to a few feet, and, since we are a little beneath them, he has got our range too. We dodge with difficulty, for Archie revels in a background of low clouds. Nobody is hit, however, and our party crosses the lines; and so home.

From the point of view of our fighting machines, the afternoon has been uneventful. Nevertheless, the job has been done, so much so that the dwellers in the wood where we left our cards are still regretting their disturbed luncheon, while airmen and A.-A. gunners around the wood tell each other what they will do to the next lot of raiders. We shall probably call on them again next week, when I will let you know whether their bloodthirsty intentions mature.

France, September, 1916

4.

Spying by Snapshot

... Since daybreak a great wind has raged from the east, and even as I write you, my best of friends, it whines past the mess-tent. This, together with low clouds, had kept aircraft inactive—a state of things in which we had revelled for nearly a week, owing to rain and mist.

However, towards late afternoon the clouds were blown from the trench region, and artillery machines snatched a few hours' work from the fag-end of daylight. The wind was too strong for offensive patrols or long reconnaissance, so that we of *Umpty* Squadron did not expect a call to flight.

But the powers that control our outgoings and incomings thought otherwise. In view of the morrow's operations they wanted urgently a plan of some new defences on which the Hun had been busy during the spell of dud weather. They selected *Umpty* Squadron for the job, probably because the Sopwith would be likely to complete it more quickly than any other type, under the adverse conditions and the time-limit set by the sinking sun. The Squadron Commander detailed two buses—ours and another.

As it was late, we had little leisure for preparation; the cameras were brought in a hurry from the photographic lorry, examined hastily by the observers who were to use them, and fitted into the conical recesses through the fuselage floor. We rose from the aerodrome within fifteen minutes of the deliverance of flying orders.

Because of doubtful light the photographs were to be taken from the comparatively low altitude of 7000 feet. We were able, therefore, to complete our climb while on the way to Albert, after meeting the second machine at 2000 feet.

All went well until we reached the neighbourhood of Albert, but there we ran into a thick ridge of cloud and became separated. We dropped below into the clear air, and hovered about in a search for the companion bus. Five minutes brought no sign of its whereabouts, so we continued alone towards the trenches. Three minutes later, when about one mile west of Pozières, we sighted, some 900 yards to north of us, a solitary machine that looked like a Sopwith, though one could not be certain at such a range. If it was indeed our second bus, its pilot, who was new to France, must have misjudged his bearings, for it nosed across to the German air country and merged into the nothingness, miles away from our objective. What became of the lost craft is a mystery which may be cleared up tomorrow, or more probably in a month's time by communication from the German Prisoners' Bureau, or maybe never. Thus far we have heard nothing, so a forced landing on British ground is unlikely. For the rest, the pilot and observer may be killed, wounded, injured, or prisoners. All we know is that they flew into the Ewigkeit and are "missing."

For these many weeks Pozières has been but a name and a waste brick pile; yet the site of the powdered village cannot be mistaken from the air, for, slightly to the east, two huge mine-craters sentinel it, left and right. From here to Le Sars, which straddles the road four miles beyond, was our photographic objective. We were to cover either side of the road twice, so I had arranged to use half the number of plates during each there-and-back journey.

The R.F.C. camera used by us is so simple as to be called foolproof. Eighteen plates are stacked in a changing-box over the shutter. You slide the loading handle forward and backward, and the first plate falls into position. Arrived over the spot to be spied upon, you take careful sight and pull a string—and the camera has reproduced whatever is 9000 feet below it. Again you operate the loading handle; the exposed plate is pushed into an empty changing-box underneath an extension, and plate the second falls into readiness for exposure, while the indicator shows 2. And so on until the changing-box for bare plates is emptied and the changing-box for used ones is filled. Whatever skill attaches to the taking of aerial snapshots is in judging when the machine is flying dead level and above the exact objective, and in repeating the process after a properly timed interval.

A.-A. guns by the dozen hit out immediately we crossed the lines, for we were their one target. No other craft were in sight, except a lone B.E., which was drifted by the wind as it spotted for artillery from the British side of the trenches. Scores of black puffs, attended by cavernous coughs, did their best to put the wind up us. They succeeded to a certain extent, though not enough to hinder the work on hand.

Everything was in Archie's favour. We were at 7000 feet—an easy height for A.-A. sighting—we were silhouetted against a cover of high clouds, our ground speed was only some thirty miles an hour against the raging wind, and we dared not dodge the bursts, however close, as area photography from anything but an even line of flight is useless. Yet, though the bursts kept us on edge, we were not touched by so much as a splinter. In this we were lucky under the conditions. The luck could scarcely have held had the job lasted much longer than a quarter of an hour—which is a consoling thought when one is safe back and writing to a dear friend in England, not?

Northward, along the left-hand side of the road, was my first subject; and a damned unpleasant subject it was—a dirty-soiled, shell-scarred wilderness. I looked overboard to make certain of the map square, withdrew back into the office, pulled the shutter-string, and loaded the next plate for exposure.

"*Wouff! Ouff! Ouff!*" barked Archie, many times and loud. An instinct to swerve assaulted the pilot, but after a slight deviation he controlled his impulse and held the bus above the roadside. He had a difficult task to maintain a level course. Whereas we wanted to make east-north-east, the wind was due east, so that it cut across and drifted us in a transverse direction. To keep straight it was necessary to steer crooked—that is to say, head three-quarters into the wind to counteract the drift, the line of flight thus forming an angle of about 12° with the longitudinal axis of the aeroplane.

"*Wouff! ouff!*" Archibald continued, as I counted in seconds the interval to the scene of the next snapshot, which, as assurance that the whole ground would be covered, was to overlap slightly the first. A quick glance below, another tug at the string, and plate the second was etched with information. The third, fourth, and fifth followed; and finally, to our great relief, we reach Le Sars.

Here the pilot was able to dodge for a few seconds while we turned to retrace the course, this time along the southern edge of the road. He side-slipped the bus, pulled it around in an Immelmann turn, and then felt the rudder-controls until we were in the required direction. The interval between successive exposures was now shorter, as the east wind brought our ground speed to 120 miles an hour, even with the engine throttled back. There was scarcely time to sight the objective before the photograph must be taken and the next plate loaded into place. Within two minutes we were again over Pozières.

V. took us across the lines, so as to deceive the Archie merchants into a belief that we were going home. We then climbed a little, turned sharply, and began to repeat our outward trip to north of the road.

Evidently Archie had allowed his leg to be pulled by the feint, and for two minutes he only molested the machine with a few wild shots. But soon he recovered his old form, so that when we had reached Le Sars the bus was again wreathed by black puffs. We vertical-turned across the road and headed for the trenches once more, with the last few plates waiting for exposure.

Archie now seemed to treat the deliberation of the solitary machine's movements as a challenge to his ability, and he determined to make us pay for our seeming contempt. An ugly barrage of A.-A. shell-bursts separated us from friendly air, the discs of black smoke expanding as they hung in little clusters. Into this barrier of hate we went unwillingly, like children sent to church as a duty.

Scores of *staccato* war-whoops reminded us that the Boche gunners wanted our scalp. I don't know how V. felt about it, but I well know that I was in a state of acute fear. Half-way to Pozières I abandoned checking the ground by the map, and judged the final photographs by counting the seconds between each—"one, two, three, four (*wouff! wouff! wouff! wouff!*)"; pull the string, press forward the loading-handle, bring it back; "one, two, three, four (*wouff! wouff! wouff! wouff!*)," *et-cetera.* Just as the final plate-number showed on the indicator a mighty report from underneath startled us, and the machine was pressed upward, left wing down.

This was terrifying enough but not harmful, for not one of the fragments from the near burst touched us, strange to say. The pilot righted the bus, and I made the last exposure, without, I am afraid, caring what patch of earth was shuttered on to the plate.

Nose down and engine full out, we hared over the trenches. Archie's hate followed for some distance, but to no purpose; and at last we were at liberty to fly home, at peace with the wind and the world. We landed less than three-quarters of an hour after we had left the aerodrome in a hurry.

"Good boys," said the Squadron Commander; "now see that lightning is used in developing your prints."

The camera was rushed to the photographic lorry, the plates were unloaded in the dark hut, the negatives were developed. Half an hour later I received the first proofs, and, with them, some degree of disappointment. Those covering the first outward and return journey between Pozières and Le Sars were good, as were the next three, at the beginning of the second journey. Then came a confused blur of superimposed ground-patterns, and at the last five results blank as the brain of a flapper. A jamb in the upper changing-box had led to five exposures on the one plate.

As you know, *mon amie,* I am a fool. But I do not like to be reminded of the self-evident fact. The photographic officer said I must have made some silly mistake with the loading handle, and he remarked sadly that the camera was supposed to be foolproof. I said he must have made some silly mistake when inspecting the camera before it left his workshop, and I remarked viciously that the camera was foolproof against a careless operator, but by no means foolproof against the careless expert. There we left the subject and the spoiled plates, as the evening was too far advanced for the trip to be repeated. As the photoman has a pleasant job at wing headquarters, whereas I am but an observer—that is to say, an R.F.C. doormat—the blame was laid on me as a matter of course. However, the information supplied by the successful exposures pleased the staff people at whose instigation the deed was done, and this was all that really mattered.

I have already told you that our main work in umpty squadron is long reconnaissance for G.H.Q. and offensive patrol. Special photographic stunts such as happened today are rare, thank the Lord. But our cameras often prepare the way for a bombing expedition. An observer returns from a reconnaissance flight with snapshots of a railhead, a busy factory, or an army headquarters. Prints are sent to the "I" people, who, at their leisure, map out in detail the point of interest. No fear of doubtful reports from the glossed surface of geometrical reproduction, for the camera, our most trusted spy, cannot distort the truth. Next a complete plan of the chosen objective, with its surroundings, is given to a bombing squadron; and finally, the pilots concerned, well primed with knowledge of exactly where to align their bombsights, fly off to destroy.

For the corps and army squadrons of the R.F.C. photography has a prominent place in the daily round. To them falls the duty of providing survey-maps of the complete system of enemy defences. Their all-seeing lenses penetrate through camouflage to new trenches and emplacements, while exposing fake fortifications. The broken or unbroken German line is fully revealed, even to such details as the barbed wire in front and the approaches in rear.

For clues to battery positions and the like, the gun country behind the frontier of the trenches is likewise searched by camera. One day a certain square on the artillery map seems lifeless. The following afternoon an overhead snapshot reveals a new clump of trees or a curious mark not to be found on earlier photographs. On the third day the mark has disappeared, or the trees are clustered in a slightly different shape. But meanwhile an exact position has been pin-pointed, so that certain heavy guns busy themselves with concentrated fire. By the fourth day the new gun-pits, or whatever it was that the Hun tried to smuggle into place unnoticed, have been demolished and is replaced by a wide rash of shell-holes.

Wonderful indeed is the record of war as preserved by prints in the archives of our photographic section. For example, we were shown last week a pair of striking snapshots taken above Martinpuich, before and after bombardment. The Before one pictured a neat little village in compact perspective of squares, rectangles, and triangles. The Aftermath pictured a tangled heap of sprawling chaos, as little like a village as is the usual popular novel like literature.

Of all the Flying Corps photographs of war, perhaps the most striking is that taken before Ypres of the first Hun gas attack. A B.E2.C., well behind the German lines, caught sight of a strange snowball of a cloud rolling across open ground, in the wake of an east wind. It flew to investigate, and the pilot photographed the phenomenon from the rear. This reproduction of a tenuous mass blown along the discoloured earth will show coming generations how the Boche introduced to the black art of warfare its most devilish form of frightfulness.

I would send you a few aerial photographs, as you suggest, if the private possession of them were not strictly *verboten*. Possibly you will have an opportunity of seeing all you want later, for if the authorities concerned are wise they will form a public collection of a few thousand representative snapshots, to show the worlds of today, tomorrow, and the day after what the camera did in the great war. Such a permanent record would be of great value to the military historian; and on a rainy afternoon, when the more vapid of the revues were not offering *matinées*, they might even be of interest to the average Londoner.

I can tell you little of the technical branch of this new science, which has influenced so largely the changing war of the past two years, and which will play an even greater part in the decisive war of the next two. All I know is that hundreds of photos are taken every day over enemy country, that ninety *per cent* of them are successful, and that the trained mechanics sometimes produce finished prints twenty minutes after we have given them our plates.

Moreover, I am not anxious to discuss the subject further, for it is 10 p.m., and at 5 a.m., unless my good angel sends bad weather, I shall be starting for an offensive patrol over Mossy-Face. Also you don't deserve even this much, as I have received no correspondence, books, or pork-pies from you for over a week. In ten minutes' time I shall be employed on the nightly slaughter of the spiders, earwigs, and moths that plague my tent. Goodnight.

France, September, 1916

5.

THE ARCHIBALD FAMILY

...You remark on the familiarity with which I speak of Archie, and you ask for detailed information about his character and habits. Why should I not treat him with familiarity? If a man calls on you nearly every day you are entitled to use his Christian name. And if the intimacy be such that at each visit he tries to punch your head, he becomes more a brother than a friend. How, you continue, did a creature so strenuous as the anti-aircraft gun come by the flippant name of Archie? Well, once upon a time the Boche A.-A. guns were very young and had all the impetuous inaccuracy incident to youth. British airmen scarcely knew they were fired at until they saw the pretty, white puffs in the distance.

One day a pilot noticed some far-away bursts, presumably meant for him. He was young enough to remember the good old days (you would doubtless call them the bad old days) when the music-halls produced hearty, if vulgar, humour, and he murmured "Archibald, certainly not!" The name clung, and as Archibald the A.-A. gun will go down to posterity. You can take it or leave it; any way, I cannot think of a better explanation for the moment.

Archie has since grown up and become sober, calculating, accurate, relentless, cunning, and deadly mathematical. John or Ernest would now fit him better, as being more serious, or Wilhelm, as being more frightful. For Archie is a true apostle of frightfulness. There is no greater adept at the gentle art of "putting the wind up" people.

Few airmen get hardened to the villainous noise of a loud *wouff! wouff!* at 12,000 feet, especially when it is near enough to be followed by the shriek of shell-fragments. Nothing disconcerts a man more as he tries to spy out the land, take photographs, direct artillery fire, or take aim through a bombsight, than to hear this noise and perhaps be lifted a hundred feet or so when a shell bursts close underneath. And one is haunted by the knowledge that, unlike the indirect fire of the more precise guns, Archie keeps his own eyes on the target and can observe all swerves and dashes for safety.

To anybody who has seen a machine broken up by a direct hit at some height between 8,000 and 15,000 feet, Archie becomes a prince among the demons of destruction. Direct hits are fortunately few, but hits by stray fragments are unfortunately many. Yet, though the damage on such occasions is regrettable, it is seldom overwhelming. Given a skilful pilot and a well-rigged bus, miracles can happen, though a machine stands no technical chance of staggering home. In the air uncommon escapes are common enough.

On several occasions, after a direct hit, a wounded British pilot has brought his craft to safety, with wings and fuselage weirdly ventilated and half the control wires helpless. Archie wounded a pilot from our aerodrome in the head and leg, and an opening the size of a duck's egg was ripped into the petrol tank facing him. The pressure went, and so did the engine-power. The lines were too distant to be reached in a glide, so the machine planed down towards Hun territory. The pilot was growing weak from loss of blood, but it occurred to him that if he stuck his knee into the hole he might be able to pump up pressure. He tried this, and the engine came back to life 50 feet from the ground. At this height he flew, in a semi-conscious condition, twelve miles over enemy country and crossed the lines with his bus scarcely touched by the dozens of machine-guns trained on it.

One of our pilots lost most of his rudder, but managed to get back by juggling with his elevator and ailerons. The fuselage of my own machine was once set on fire by a chunk of burning H.E. The flames died out under pressure from gloves and hands, just as they had touched the drums of ammunition and all but eaten through a longeron.

Escapes from personal injuries have been quite as strange. A piece of high explosive hit a machine sideways, passed right through the observer's cockpit, and grazed two kneecaps belonging to a friend of mine. He was left with nothing worse than two cuts and mild shell-shock.

Scottie, another observer (now a prisoner, poor chap), leaned forward to look at his map while on a reconnaissance. A dainty morsel from an Archie shell hurtled through the air and grazed the back of his neck. He finished the reconnaissance, made out his report, and got the scratch dressed at the hospital. Next day he resumed work; and he was delighted to find himself in the Roll of Honour, under the heading "Wounded." I once heard him explain to a new observer that when flying a close study of the map was a guarantee against losing one's way, one's head—and one's neck.

The Archibald family tree has several branches. Whenever the founder of the family went on the burst he broke out in the form of white puffs, like those thrown from the funnel of a liner when it begins to slow down. The white bursts still seek us out, but the modern Boche A.-A. gunner specialises more in the black variety. The white bursts contain shrapnel, which is cast outwards and upwards; the black ones contain high explosive, which spreads all around.

H.E. has a lesser radius of solid frightfulness than shrapnel, but if it does hit a machine the damage is greater. For vocal frightfulness the black beat the white hollow. If the Titans ever had an epidemic of whooping-cough, and a score of them chorused the symptoms in unison, I should imagine the noise was like the bursting of a black Archie shell.

Then there is the green branch of the family. This is something of a problem. One theory is that the green bursts are for ranging purposes only, another that they contain a special brand of H.E., and a third declares them to be gas shells. All three suggestions may be partly true, for there is certainly more than one brand of green Archie.

First cousin to Archie is the onion, otherwise the flaming rocket. It is fired in a long stream of what look like short rectangles of compressed flame at machines that have been enticed down to a height of 4000 to 6000 feet. It is most impressive as a firework display. There are also colourless phosphorous rockets that describe a wide parabola in their flight.

Within the past month or two we have been entertained at rare intervals by the family ghost. This fascinating and mysterious being appears very suddenly in the form of a pillar of white smoke, stretching to a height of several thousand feet. It is straight, and apparently rigid as far as the top, where it sprays round into a knob. Altogether, it suggests a giant piece of celery. It does not seem to disperse; but if you pass on and look away for a quarter of an hour, you will find on your return that it has faded away as suddenly as it came, after the manner of ghosts. Whether the pillars are intended to distribute gas is uncertain, but it is a curious fact that on the few occasions when we have seen them they have appeared to windward of us.

Like babies and lunatics, Archie has his good and bad days. If low clouds are about and he can only see through the gaps he is not very troublesome. Mist also helps to keep him quiet. He breaks out badly when the sky is a cover of unbroken blue, though the sun sometimes dazzles him, so that he fires amok. From his point of view it is a perfect day when a film of cloud about 20,000 feet above him screens the sky. The high clouds forms a perfect background for anything between it and the ground, and aircraft stand out boldly, like the figures on a Greek vase. On such a day we would willingly change places with the gunners below.

For my part, Archie has given me a fellow-feeling for the birds of the air. I have at times tried light-heartedly to shoot partridges and even pigeons, but if ever again I fire at anything on the wing, sympathy will spoil my aim.

France, October, 1916

6.

BATTLES AND BULLETS

... I am not sure which is the more disquieting, to be under fire in the air or on the ground.

Although the airman is less likely to be hit than the infantryman, he has to deal with complications that could not arise on solid earth. Like the infantryman, a pilot may be killed outright by a questing bullet, and there's an end of it. But in the case of a wound he has a far worse time. If an infantryman be plugged he knows he has probably received "a Blighty one," and as he is taken to the dressing-station he dreams of spending next weekend in England. A wounded pilot dare think of nothing but to get back to safety with his machine, and possibly an observer.

He may lose blood and be attacked by a paralysing faintness. He must then make his unwilling body continue to carry out the commands of his unwilling brain, for if he gives way to unconsciousness the machine, freed from reasoned control, will perform circus tricks and twist itself into a spinning nose-dive. Even when he has brought the bus to friendly country he must keep clear-headed; otherwise he will be unable to exercise the judgment necessary for landing.

Another unpleasant thought is that though he himself escape unhurt, an incendiary bullet may set his petrol tank ablaze, or some stray shots may cut his most vital control wires. And a headlong dive under these conditions is rather too exciting, even for the most confirmed seeker after sensation.

Yet with all these extra possibilities of what a bullet may mean, the chances of being plugged in the air are decidedly less than on the ground. While travelling at anything from 70 to 140 miles an hour it is decidedly more difficult to hit another object tearing along at a like speed and swerving in all directions, than from a machine-gun emplacement to rake a line of men advancing "over the top." Another point favourable to the airman is that he scarcely realises the presence of bullets around him, for the roar of his engine drowns that sinister hiss which makes a man automatically close his eyes and duck.

Given a certain temperament and a certain, mood, an air fight is the greatest form of sport on earth. Every atom of personality, mental and physical, is conscripted into the task. The brain must be instinctive with insight into the enemy's moves, and with plans to check and outwit him. The eye must cover every direction and co-operate with the brain in perfect judgments of time and distance. Hands, fingers, and feet must be instantaneous in seizing an opportunity to swoop and fire, swerve and avoid, retire and return.

In an isolated fight between two single machines the primary aim of each pilot is to attack by surprise at close quarters. If this be impossible, he plays for position and tries to get above his opponent. He opens fire first if he can, as this may disconcert the enemy, but he must be careful not to waste ammunition at long range. A machine with little ammunition is at a tremendous disadvantage against a machine with plenty.

If an isolated British aeroplane sees a formation of Germans crossing to our side it has no hesitation in sweeping forward to break up the party. You will remember our old friend Marmaduke, dear lady? Only last week he attacked ten German machines, chased them back to their own place in the air, and drove two down.

Even from the purely selfish point of view much depends on the area. When an airman destroys a Boche over German country he may have no witnesses, in which case his report is attended by an elusive shadow of polite doubt. But if the deed be done near the trenches, his success is seen by plenty of people

195

only too willing to support his claim. Sometimes a pilot may even force a damaged Boche machine to land among the British. He then follows his captive down, receives the surrender, and wonders if he deserves the Military Cross or merely congratulations.

The tactics of an air battle on a larger scale are much more complicated than those for single combats. A pilot must be prepared at every instant to change from the offensive to the defensive and back again, to take lightning decisions, and to extricate himself from one part of the fight and sweep away to another, if by so doing he can save a friend or destroy an enemy.

To help you realise some of the experiences of an air battle, my very dear madam, let us suppose you have changed your sex and surroundings, and are one of us, flying in a bunch over the back of the German front, seeking whom we may devour.

A moment ago the sky was clear of everything but those dainty cloud-banks to the east. Very suddenly a party of enemies appear out of nowhere, and we rush to meet them. Like the rest of us, you concentrate your whole being on the part you must play, and tune yourself up to the strain attendant on the first shock of encounter. What happens in the first few seconds often decides the fight.

The opposing forces close up and perfect their order of battle. The usual German method, during the past few weeks, has been to fly very high and range the machines one above the other. If the higher craft are in trouble they dive and join the others. If one of the lower ones be surrounded those above can swoop down to its help. Our own tactics vary according to circumstances.

At the start it is a case of follow-my-leader. The flight-commander selects a Boche and dives straight at him. You follow until you are within range, then swerve away and around, so as to attack from the side. Then, with a clear field, you pour in a raking fire by short bursts—*ta-ta-ta-ta, ta-ta-ta-ta-ta, ta-ta-ta-ta*, aiming to hit the Boche pilot and allowing for deflection. From all directions you hear the rattle of other guns, muffled by the louder noise of the engine.

A third British machine is under the Boche's tail, and the observer in it is firing upwards. The three of you draw nearer and nearer to your prey. The Hun puts his nose down to sweep away; but it is too late. His petrol tank bursts into flames, and the machine dives steeply, a streamer of flame running away behind it. The fire spreads to the fuselage and planes. After rushing earthwards for two or three thousand feet, the whole aeroplane crumbles up and you see the main portion falling like a stone. And you (who have shed the skin of sentiment and calm restraint and become for the duration of the fight a bold bad pilot with the lust of battle in your blood) are filled with joy.

Meanwhile, your observer's gun has been grinding away behind you, showing that you in your turn are attacked. You twist the machine round. Almost instinctively your feet push the rudder-control just sufficiently to let you aim dead at the nearest enemy. You press the trigger. Two shots are fired, and—your gun jambs.

You bank and turn sideways, so as to let your observer get in some shooting while you examine your gun. From the position of the check-lever you realise that there has been a misfire. Quickly but calmly—feverish haste might make a temporary stoppage chronic—you lean over and remedy the fault. Again you press the trigger, and never was sound more welcome than the *ta-ta-ta-ta-ta* which shows you are ready for all comers.

Once more you turn to meet the attacking Germans. As you do so your observer points to a black-crossed bird which is gliding down after he has crippled it. But three more are closing round you. Something sings loudly a yard away. You turn your head and see that a landing wire has been shot through; and you thank the gods that it was not a flying wire.

The flight-commander and another companion have just arrived to help you. They dash at a Boche, and evidently some of their shots reach him, for he also separates himself and glides down. The two other Huns, finding themselves outnumbered, retire.

All this while the two rear machines have been having a bad time. They were surrounded by five enemies at the very beginning of the fight. One of the Boches has since disappeared, but the other four are very much there.

You sweep round and go to the rescue, accompanied by the flight-commander and the remaining British machine. Just as you arrive old X's bus drops forward and down, spinning as it goes. It falls slowly at first, but seems to gather momentum; the

197

spin becomes wilder and wilder, the drop faster and faster.

"Poor old X," you think, "how damnable to lose him. Now the poor beggar won't get the leave he has been talking about for the last two months." Then your thoughts turn to Y, the observer in the lost machine. You know his *fiancée*, you remember he owes you 30 francs from last night's game of bridge.

You burn to avenge poor X and Y, but all the Huns have dived and are now too low for pursuit. You recover your place in the formation and the fight ends as suddenly as it began. One German machine has been destroyed and two driven down, but— "one of ours has failed to return."

When you return and land, you are not so contented as usual to be back. There will be two vacant places at dinner, and there is a nasty job to be done. You will have to write rather a painful letter to Y's *fiancée*.

Madam, you are now at liberty to give up the temporary role of a bold, bad pilot and become once more your charming self.

France, November, 1916

7.

BACK IN BLIGHTY

. . . You last heard of my continued existence, I believe, from a field postcard with but one of the printed lines uncrossed: "I have been admitted to hospital." When this was sent I had no more expectation of a return to Blighty than has a rich Bishop of not entering the Kingdom of Heaven. Nevertheless, here we are again, after a three days' tour along the Red Cross lines of communication.

Again I have been admitted to hospital. This one is more sumptuous but less satisfying than the casualty clearing station at Gezaincourt, whence the card was posted. There, in a small *château* converted into an R.A.M.C. half-way house, one was not over-anxious to be up and about, for that would have meant a further dose of war at close quarters. Here, in a huge military hospital at Westminster, one is very anxious to be up and about, for that would mean a long-delayed taste of the joys of London. At Gezaincourt rumbling gunfire punctuated the countryside stillness; aeroplanes hummed past on their way to the lines, and engendered gratitude for a respite from encounters with Archie; from the ward window I could see the star-shells as they streaked up through the dim night. At Westminster rumbling buses punctuate the back-street stillness; taxis hum past on their way to the West End, and engender a longing for renewed acquaintance with the normal world and the normal devil; from the ward window I can see the towers of Parliament as they stretch up through the London greyness. For an Englishman just returned from a foreign battlefield to his own capital it should be an inspiring view, that of the Home of Government, wherein the Snowdens, Outhwaites, Ponsonbys, and Sir Vested Interests, talk their hardest for the winning of the war by one side or the other, I am not sure which. But somehow it isn't.

I have mentioned the hospital's position, because it will help you on the day after tomorrow, if the herewith forecast is correct.

You will read this letter, hang me for my customary disturbing suddenness, and search a time-table. This will tell you that a train from your part of the country arrives in town at 11.45 a.m. (e), which bracketed letter means Saturdays excepted. By it you will travel on Tuesday morning. Then, in the afternoon, you will seek a taxi, but either the drivers will have as fares middle-aged contractors, good for a fat tip, or they will claim a lack of petrol, lady. You will therefore fight for place in a bus, which must be left at the corner of Whitehall and Queen Victoria Street. Next you will walk towards the river, past Westminster Abbey and the Houses of Talk, and so to Chelsea Embankment. Turn off by the Tate Gallery, enter the large building on your right, and you will have arrived. Visiting hours are from two to four, but as the Sister is one of the best and my very kind friend, you will not be turned out until five.

But I can hear you ask leading questions. No, I am not badly wounded nor seriously ill. Neither am I suffering from shell-shock, nor even from cold feet. A Blighty injury of the cushiest is the spring actuating this Jack-in-the-Box appearance. Have patience. Today's inactivity has bred a pleasant boredom, which I shall work off by writing you a history of the reasons why I am back from the big war. They include a Hun aeroplane, a crash, a lobster, and two doctors.

You will remember how, months ago, our machine landed on an abandoned trench, after being damaged in a scrap? A bullet through the petrol-pipe having put the carburettor out of action, the engine ceased its revs., so that we glided several miles, crossed the then lines at a low height, and touched earth among the network of last June's lines. We pancaked on to the far edge of a trench, and the wheels slid backward into the cavity, causing the lower wings and fuselage to be crumpled and broken.

My left knee, which has always been weak since a far-back accident, was jerked by contact with the parapet. Next day it seemed none the worse, so I did not take the accident seriously. During the weeks and months that followed the knee was painless, but it grew larger and larger for no noticeable reason, like Alice in Wonderland and the daily cost of the war.

Then an aggressive lobster, eaten in Amiens one fine evening, revenged itself by making necessary a visit to the casualty clearing station for attention to a mildly poisoned tummy. The doctor who examined me noticed the swollen knee, and looked grave. He pinched, punched, and pressed it, and finally said: "My dear boy, why the devil didn't you report this? It's aggravated synovitis, and, if you don't want permanent water-on-the-knee, you'll have to lie up for at least three weeks. I'll have you sent to the Base tomorrow."

My ambition did not yet soar beyond a short rest at the Base. Meanwhile it was pleasant to lie between real sheets and to watch real English girls making beds, taking temperatures, and looking after the newly wounded with a blend of tenderness and masterful competence. Their worst job appeared to be fighting the Somme mud. The casualties from the trench region were invariably caked with dirt until the nurses had bathed and cleaned them with comic tact and great success.

It being the day of an advance, scores of cases were sent to Gezaincourt from the field dressing stations. Each time an ambulance car, loaded with broken and nerve-shattered men, stopped by the hospital entrance, a young donkey brayed joyously from a field facing the doorway, as if to shout *"Never say die!"* Most of the casualties echoed the sentiment, for they seemed full of beans and congratulated themselves and each other on their luck in getting Blighty ones. But it was otherwise with the cases of shell-shock. I can imagine no more wretched state of mind than that of a man whose nerves have just been unbalanced by close shaves from gun fire. There was in the same lysol-scented ward as myself a New Zealander in this condition. While he talked with a friend a shell had burst within a few yards of the pair, wounding him in the thigh and sweeping off the friend's head. He lost much blood and became a mental wreck. All day and all night he tossed about in his bed, miserably sleepless and acutely on edge, or lay in a vacant and despondent quiet. Nothing interested him, nothing comforted him—not even a promise from the doctor of a long rest in England.

There were also many victims of the prevailing epidemics of trench-fever and rabid influenza. The clearing station was thus hard put to it to make room for all newcomers by means of evacuation. For our batch this happened next evening. A long train drew up on the single-line railway near the hospital, the stretcher cases were borne to special Pullman cars, and the walking cases followed, each docketed in his button-hole by a card descriptive of wound or ailment.

You can have no idea of the comfort of a modern R.A.M.C. train as used at the Front. During the first few months of war, when the small amount of available rolling stock was worth its weight in man-power, the general travel accommodation for the wounded was the French railway truck, with straw strewn over the floor. In these the suffering sick were jolted, jerked, and halted for hours at a time, while the scorching sun danced through the van's open sides and the mosquito-flies bit their damnedest. But nowadays one travels in luxury and sleeping-berths, with ever-ready nurses eager to wait upon every whim. A sling-armed Canadian was one of the party of four in our compartment. Great was his joy when a conjuring trick of co-incidence revealed that the jolly sister who came to ask what we would like to drink proved to be not only a Canadian, but actually from his own little township in Manitoba. While they discussed mutual friends the rest of us felt highly disappointed that we also were not from the township. As evidence that they both were of the right stuff, neither of them platitudinised: "*It's a small world, isn't it?*"

The smooth-running train sped northward from the Somme battlefield, and we betted on each man's chances of being sent to Blighty. Before settling down to sleep, we likewise had a sweepstake on the Base of destination, for not until arrival were we told whether it was Rouen, Boulogne, or Etaples. I drew Boulogne and won, as we discovered on being awoken at early dawn by a nurse, who arrived with tea, a cheery "Morning, boys," and bread-and-butter thin as ever was poised between your slim fingers.

The wounded and shell-shocked New Zealander had pegged out during the journey. May the gods rest his troubled spirit!

From Boulogne station a fleet of ambulance cars distributed the train's freight of casualties among the various general hospitals. At three of the starry morning I found myself inside a large one-time hotel on the sea front, being introduced to a bed by a deft-handed nurse of unusual beauty.

The Blighty hopes of our party were realised or disappointed at midday, when the surgeon-in-charge came to decide which of the new arrivals were to be forwarded across Channel, and which were to be patched up in France. The world stands still the moment before the Ram Corps major, his examination concluded, delivers the blessed verdict: "Get him off by this afternoon's boat, sister." Or an unwelcome reassurance: "We'll soon get you right here."

For my part I had not the least expectation of Blighty until the surgeon showed signs of prolonged dissatisfaction with the swollen knee. Like the doctor at Gezaincourt, he pinched, punched, and pressed it, asked for its history, and finally pronounced: "I'm afraid it'll have to be rested for about six weeks." Then, after a pause: "Sorry we haven't room to keep you here for so long. You'll be fixed up on the other side." Hastily I remarked that I should be sorry indeed to take up valuable space at a Base hospital. The major's departure from the ward was the signal for a demonstration by the Blighty squad. Pillows and congratulations were thrown about, war-dances were performed on game legs, the sister was bombarded with inquiries about the next boat.

All places on the afternoon boat having been booked, we were obliged to wait until the morning. What a day! The last of a long period amid the myriad *ennuies* of active service, the herald of a long spell amid the pleasant things of England. Impatience for the morrow was kept bottled with difficulty; every now and then the cork flew out, resulting in a wild rag among those able to run, walk, or hop. When the *Times* was delivered, it seemed quite a minor matter that the *Gazette* should notify me that I had been presented with another pip.

After dinner someone remarked that "she" would soon come on duty, and there was an air of conscious expectancy among the veterans of the ward. "She," the V.A.D. girl who had received us when we were deposited at the hospital in the small hours of the morning, was—and is—an efficient nurse, a good comrade, a beautiful woman, and the friend of every casualty lucky enough to have been in her charge. For a wounded officer staled by the brutalities of trench life there could be no better mental tonic than the ministrations and charm of Our Lady of X Ward. I cannot guess the number and variety of proposals made to her by patients of a week's or a month's standing, but both must be large. She is also the possessor of this admirable and remarkable record. For two years she has been nursing—really nursing—in France, and yet, though she belongs to a well-known family, her photograph has never appeared in the illustrated papers that boom war-work patriots. On this particular evening, in the intervals of handing round medicines and cheerfulness, our comrade the night nurse made toffee for us over a gas-burner, a grey-haired colonel and a baby subaltern taking turns to stir the saucepan.

The next change of scene was to the quays of Boulogne. Ambulance cars from the several hospitals lined up before a ship side-marked by giant Red Crosses. The stretcher casualties were carried up the gangway, down the stairs, and into the boat's wards below. The remainder were made comfortable on deck. Distribution of life-saving contraptions, business with medical cards, gleeful hoots from the funnel, chug-chug from the paddles, and hey for Blighty! across a smooth lake of a sea. Yarns of attack and bombardment were interrupted by the pleasurable discovery that Dover's cliffs were still white.

We seemed an unkempt crowd indeed by contrast with dwellers on this side of the Channel. The ragged raiment of men pipped during a Somme advance did not harmonise with plush first-class compartments of the Chatham and Dover railway. Every uniform in our carriage, except mine and another, was muddied and bloodied, so that I felt almost ashamed of the comparative cleanliness allowed by life in an R.F.C. camp, miles behind the lines. The subaltern opposite, however, was immaculate as the fashion-plate of a Sackville Street tailor. Yet, we thought, he must have seen some tough times, for he knew all about each phase of the Somme operations. Beaumont Hamel? He explained exactly how the Blankshires and Dashshires, behind a dense barrage, converged up the high ground fronting the stronghold. Stuff Redoubt? He gave us a complete account of its capture, loss, and recapture. But this seasoned warrior quietened after the visit of an official who listed us with particulars of wounds, units, and service. His service overseas? Five months in the Claims Department at Amiens. Wound or sickness? Scabies.

Charing Cross, gateway of the beloved city! The solid old clock looked down benignly as if to say: "I am the first landmark of your own London to greet you. Pass along through that archway and greet the others."

But we could not pass along. The medical watchdogs and *mesdemoiselles* the ambulance-drivers saw to that. We were detailed to cars and forwarded to the various destinations, some to the provinces by way of another station, some to suburban hospitals, some to London proper. I was one of the lucky lastnamed and soon found myself settled in Westminster. Here the injured knee was again pinched, punched, and pressed, after which the ward surgeon told me I should probably stay in bed for a month. For exercise I shall be permitted to walk along the passage each morning to the department where they dispense massage and ionisation.

Meanwhile, it is midday and flying weather. Over there a formation of A flight, *Umpty* Squadron, will perhaps be droning back from a hundred-mile reconnaissance. V., my mad friend and sane pilot and flight-commander, leads it; and in my place, alas! Charlie-the-good-guide is making notes from the observer's cockpit. The Tripehound and others of the jolly company man the rear buses, which number four or five, according to whether the wicked bandit Missing has kidnapped some member of the family. And here loaf I, uncertain whether I am glad or sorry to be out of it. The devil of it is that, unlike most of my bed-neighbours, I feel enormously fit and am anxious to shake hands with life and London. Time hangs heavy and long, so bring all you can in the way of the latest books, the latest scandals, and your latest enthusiasms among the modern poets. Above all, bring yourself.

London, November, 1916